MW00389412

DEEPENING
LIFE
TOGETHER

**PROMISES
OF GOD**

LIFE TOGETHER

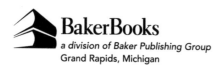

BakerBooks
a division of Baker Publishing Group
Grand Rapids, Michigan

© 2009 by Lifetogether Publishing

Published by Baker Books
a division of Baker Publishing Group
P.O. Box 6287, Grand Rapids, MI 49516-6287
www.bakerbooks.com

Printed in the United States of America

Library of Congress Cataloging-in-Publication Data
Promises of God / [editors, Mark L. Strauss, Teresa Haymaker].
    p.   cm. — (Deepening life together)
  Includes bibliographical references.
  ISBN 978-0-8010-6848-5 (pbk.)
  1. God—Promises—Textbooks. 2. God—Promises—Study and teaching. I. Strauss, Mark L. II. Haymaker, Teresa.
  BT180.P7P76 2009
  231.7—dc22   2009014855

CONTENTS

Contents

ACKNOWLEDGMENTS

The *Deepening Life Together: Promises of God* Small Group Video Bible Study has come together through the efforts of many at Baker Publishing Group, Lifetogether Publishing, and Lamplighter Media, for which we express our heartfelt thanks.

Executive Producer	John Nill
Producer and Director	Sue Doc Ross
Editors	Mark L. Strauss (Scholar), Teresa Haymaker
Curriculum Development	Brett Eastman, Pam Marotta, Sue Doc Ross, Stephanie French, Teresa Haymaker, Virgil Hurley, Mark L. Strauss, Karen Lee-Thorp
Video Production	Chris Balish, Rodney Bissell, Nick Calabrese, Sebastian Hoppe Fuentes, Josh Greene, Patrick Griffin, Teresa Haymaker, Oziel Jabin Ibarra, Natali Ibarra, Janae Janik, Keith Sorrell, Lance Tracy
Teachers and Scholars	Andrew Hill, Joanne Jung, Dennis Keating, Mark Strauss, David Talley, Eric Thoennes, Daniel Watson
Baker Publishing Group	Jack Kuhatschek

Special thanks to DeLisa Ivy, Bethel Seminary, Talbot School of Theology, Wheaton College

Clips from The JESUS Film are copyright © 1995–2009 The JESUS Film Project®. A ministry of Campus Crusade for Christ International®.

Interior icons by Tom Clark

READ ME FIRST

Most people want to live a healthy, balanced spiritual life, but few achieve this by themselves. And most small groups struggle to balance all of God's purposes in their meetings. Groups tend to overemphasize one of the five purposes, perhaps fellowship or discipleship. Rarely is there a healthy balance that includes evangelism, ministry, and worship. That's why we've included all of these elements in this study so you can live a healthy, balanced spiritual life over time.

A typical group session will include the following:

Memory Verses

For each session we have provided a memory verse that emphasizes an important truth from the session. This is an optional exercise, but we believe that memorizing Scripture can be a vital part of filling our minds with God's Word. We encourage you to give this important habit a try.

 CONNECTING *with God's Family (Fellowship)*

The foundation for spiritual growth is an intimate connection with God and his family. A few people who really know you and who earn

7

your trust provide a place to experience the life Jesus invites you to live. This section of each session typically offers you two activities. You can get to know your whole group by using the icebreaker question, and/or you can check in with one or two group members—your spiritual partner(s)—for a deeper connection and encouragement in your spiritual journey.

DVD TEACHING SEGMENT. A *Deepening Life Together: Promises of God* Video Teaching DVD companion to this study guide is available. For each study session, the DVD contains a lesson taught by Dennis Keating. If you are using the DVD, you will view the teaching segment after your *Connecting* discussion and before your group discussion time (the *Growing* section). At the end of each session in this study guide you will find space for your notes on the teaching segment.

GROWING *to Be Like Christ (Discipleship)*

Here is where you come face-to-face with Scripture. In core passages you'll explore what the Bible teaches about the topic of the study. The focus won't be on accumulating information but on how we should live in light of the Word of God. We want to help you apply the Scriptures practically, creatively, and from your heart as well as your head. At the end of the day, allowing the timeless truths from God's Word to transform our lives in Christ is our greatest aim.

DEVELOPING *Your Gifts to Serve Others (Ministry)*

Jesus trained his disciples to discover and develop their gifts to serve others. And God has designed each of us uniquely to serve him in a way no other person can. This section will help you discover and use your God-given design. It will also encourage your group to discover your unique design as a community. In this study, you'll put into practice what you've learned in the Bible study by taking a step to serve others. These simple steps will take your group on a faith journey that could change your lives forever.

SHARING *Your Life Mission Every Day (Evangelism)*

Many people skip over this aspect of the Christian life because it's scary, relationally awkward, or simply too much work for their busy schedules. But Jesus wanted all of his disciples to help outsiders connect with him, to know him personally. This doesn't mean preaching on street corners. It could mean welcoming a few newcomers into your group, hosting a short-term group in your home, or walking through this study with a friend. In this study, you'll have an opportunity to go beyond Bible study to biblical living.

SURRENDERING *Your Life for God's Pleasure (Worship)*

God is most pleased by a heart that is fully his. Each group session will give you a chance to surrender your heart to God in prayer and worship. You may read a psalm together, share a page in your journal, or sing a song to close your meeting. If you have never prayed aloud in a group before, no one will pressure you. Instead, you'll experience the support of others who are praying for you.

Study Notes

This section provides background notes on the Bible passage(s) you examine in the *Growing* section. You may want to refer to these notes during your group meeting or as a reference for those doing additional study.

For Deeper Study (Optional)

If you want to dig deeper into more Bible passages about the topic at hand, we've provided additional passages and questions. Your group may choose to do study homework ahead of each meeting in order to cover more biblical material. Or you as an individual may choose to study the *For Deeper Study* on your own. If you prefer not to do study homework, the *Growing* section will provide you with plenty to discuss within the group. These options allow individuals or the whole group to go deeper in their study, while still accommodating those who can't do homework or are new to your group.

You can record your discoveries in your journal. We encourage you to read some of your insights to a friend (spiritual partner) for accountability and support. Spiritual partners may check in each week over the phone, through e-mail, or at the beginning of the group meeting.

Reflections

On the *Reflections* pages we provide Scriptures to read and reflect on between group meetings. We suggest you use this section to seek God at home throughout the week. This time at home should begin and end with prayer. Don't get in a hurry; take enough time to hear God's direction.

Subgroup for Discussion and Prayer

If your group is large (more than seven people), we encourage you to separate into groups of two to four for discussion and prayer. This is to encourage greater participation and deeper discussion.

INTRODUCTION

Welcome to the *Deepening Life Together* Bible study on the *Promises of God*. As we live this Bible study experience together, we will unpack principles from God's Word that reveal the faithfulness of God to keep his promises. The journey you are about to embark on will take you step-by-step through God's unfolding promise to restore humanity to perfect relationship with him through Abraham, David, and eventually through his son, Jesus Christ. As you read, discuss, and reflect on the topic of each session, your confidence in God's faithfulness will grow to new heights.

This journey will connect you with our loving and faithful God and with other believers. For some of you, this might be the first time you've connected in a small group community. We want you to know that God cares about you and your spiritual growth. As you prayerfully respond to the principles you learn in this study, God will move you to a deeper level of commitment and intimacy with himself, as well as with those in your small group.

We at Baker Books and Lifetogether Publishing look forward to hearing the stories of how God changes you from the inside out during this small group experience. We pray God blesses you with all he has planned for you through this journey together.

> For the LORD is good and his love endures forever;
> his faithfulness continues through all generations.
>
> Psalm 100:5 (NIV)

11

THE PROMISE INITIATED

Memory Verse: And I will put enmity between you and the woman, and between your offspring and hers; he will crush your head, and you will strike his heel (Gen. 3:15 NIV).

It is impossible for humanity to know what the world once was prior to sin. While we may be able to imagine God's creation before the Fall, without absolute knowledge of his original design, our imperfect imaginations fall short of God's perfection.

We will get to see God's creation in all its intended glory one day. But until then, we must wait in our present, imperfect condition. Thankfully, because God is faithful to keep his promises, we don't have to wait alone.

Today, we will learn about not only the consequences of Adam and Eve's sin on creation, but also God's subsequent promise to restore humanity to its unfallen state in perfect relationship with him. In the weeks to come, as we see God's plan for the fulfillment of his promise revealed, we will be assured that he keeps his promises today.

Connecting

Begin your group time with prayer. Ask God to open your hearts to receive his Word through this Bible study and for the courage to change as he challenges you in the weeks to come.

Deeper relationships happen when we take the time to keep in touch with one another. As you begin, pass around a copy of the *Small Group Roster*, a sheet of paper, or one of you pass your study guide, opened to the *Small Group Roster*. When the roster gets to you write down your contact information, including the best time and method for contacting you. Then, someone volunteer to make copies or type up a list with everyone's information and e-mail it to the group this week.

1. Begin this first session by introducing yourselves. Include your name, what you do for a living, and what you do for fun. You may also include whether or not you are married, how long you have been married, how many children you have, and their ages. Also share what brought you to this small group study of the *Promises of God* and what you expect to learn during the next seven sessions.

2. Whether your group is new or ongoing, it's always important to reflect on and review your values together. In the *Appendix* is a *Small Group Agreement* with the values most useful in sustaining healthy, balanced groups. Choose two or three values that you have room to grow in, or haven't previously focused on, to emphasize during this study. Doing this will take your group to the next stage of intimacy and spiritual health.

    If your group is new, you may want to focus on welcoming newcomers or on sharing group ownership. Any group will quickly move from being "the leader's group" to "our group" if everyone understands the goals of the group and shares a small role. See the *Team Roles* in the *Appendix* for help on how to do this well.

3. Think about what a perfect world might be like, and respond briefly to one of the following questions (each group member may choose one):

☐ What would a perfect world look like?

☐ How would people behave?

☐ Where would you live?

☐ What would you do with your time?

Growing

To complete his perfect creation, God places Adam and Eve in the garden of Eden to live in a harmonious relationship with one another and with him. When Adam and Eve rebel against God, his perfect justice demands that he punish them for their sin. Yet in the midst of judgment, God promises that one day he will crush the power of Satan and restore the relationship.

Read Genesis 2:4–25.

4. In 2:15–17, how does God restrict Adam when he places him in the garden?

5. What do you learn about God from 2:7–10, 15–18?

Read Genesis 3:1–24.

6. What do you learn about the serpent (Satan) in 3:1–5?

7. See the *Study Notes* for insight into the tree of the knowledge of good and evil. How does Satan go about tempting Eve to eat from the forbidden tree (3:1, 4–5)?

Why do you think Satan chooses this particular approach?

8. After Adam and Eve eat the fruit, they immediately realize the gravity of their sin and hide in shame (3:7–10). How is Adam

and Eve's reaction to the revelation of their sin similar to our own reactions to wrongdoing today?

9. God seeks out Adam and Eve, asking, "Where are you?" Does God do this when you sin? What does this say about God's character?

10. What is the significance of Adam and Eve's realization of their nakedness (3:7; compare 2:25)?

11. God clearly cares about Adam and Eve in Genesis 3:14–24, so why do you think he follows through by judging them and not only Satan?

12. Look at the judgments God declares upon Adam, Eve, Satan, and all creation in the table below. How do you see each one manifesting itself in society today?

God's Judgments

Adam	Eve	Satan	Creation
Hard work to survive (v. 19)	Pain in childbirth (v. 16a)	Cursed (v. 14)	The ground is cursed to be less fertile (vv. 17–18)
Eventual physical death (v. 19)	Desire . . . rule by husband (v. 16b)	Enmity between him and Eve's descendant (v. 15)	

13. When Adam and Eve rebel against God, his perfect justice demands that he impose the promised consequences for their sin. Yet in the midst of that judgment, God makes another promise. See the *Study Notes* for the meaning of the "seed" in 3:15 and the Fall.

    What promise does God make in 3:15? What do you think this means?

14. Why is it important for God to banish Adam and Eve from the garden (3:22–23)?

15. What does this story of command, sin, judgment, and promise have to do with you?

Although Adam and Eve were created to live in a perfect relationship with God, they chose to disobey him and reject his authority in their lives. To meet the demands of his own perfect justice, God judged them for that sin, and Adam and Eve, and all of creation, entered into a fallen state. While pronouncing judgment against the serpent who tempted them, God promised that one day a descendant ("seed") of the woman would break the power of Satan, sin, and death and would restore humanity to its intended perfect relationship with God.

 Developing

God created us to serve him and has given every believer special gifts to be used in service as the Holy Spirit leads. The first step in developing the gifts that God has given each of us, is to deepen our relationship with him through prayer, reflection, and meditation on his Word. Through these disciplines, we learn how to hear his voice and submit to the leading of the Holy Spirit.

16. Developing our ability to serve God according to the leading of the Holy Spirit requires that we make time to let God speak to us daily. Which of the following next steps toward this goal are you willing to take for the next few weeks?

☐ *Prayer.* Commit to connecting with God daily through personal prayer. It's important to separate yourself from the distractions in your life so you can really focus on communicating with God. Some people find it helpful to write out their prayers in a journal.

☐ *Reflection.* At the end of each session you'll find *Reflections* Scriptures that specifically relate to the topic of our study for the session. These are provided to give you an opportunity for reading a short Bible passage five days a week during the course of this study. Write down your insights on what you read each day in the space provided. On the sixth day, summarize what God has shown you throughout the week.

☐ *Meditation.* Psalm 119:11 says: "I have hidden your word in my heart that I might not sin against you" (NIV). Meditation is focused attention on the Word of God and is a great way to internalize God's Word more deeply. One way to do this is to write a portion of Scripture on a card and tape it somewhere where you're sure to see it often, such as your bathroom mirror, car's dashboard, or the kitchen table. Think about it as you get dressed in the morning, when you sit at red lights, or while you're eating a meal. Reflect on what God is saying to you through his words. Consider using the passages provided in the *Reflections* pages in each session. As you meditate upon these Scriptures, you will notice them beginning to take up residence in your heart and mind.

Sharing

Jesus lived and died so that mankind might come to know him and be reconciled to God through him. His final words before his ascension recorded in Acts 1:8 were: "You will receive power when the Holy Spirit comes on you; and you will be my witnesses in Jerusalem, and in all Judea and Samaria, and to the ends of the earth" (NIV). Through the Holy Spirit, we are empowered to be his witnesses to those around us.

17. Jesus wants all of his disciples to help others connect with him, to know him personally. In the weeks to come, you'll be asked to identify and share with people in your circle of influence who need to know Jesus or need to connect with him through a small group community. With this in mind, as you go about your day-to-day activities this week, pay special attention to the people God has placed in your life. There may be co-workers, family or friends, other parents at school or sporting events that you see or talk to on a regular basis. When we meet next time, we'll talk about how to help connect believers to Chris-

tian community and begin sharing Jesus with those who don't yet know him.

Surrendering

God wants us to turn our hearts to him. Second Chronicles 16:9 says: "The eyes of the LORD search the whole earth in order to strengthen those whose hearts are fully committed to him" (NLT). Each week you will have a chance to surrender your hearts to God in worship and prayer.

18. Every believer should have a plan for spending time alone with God. Your time with God is personal and reflects who you are in relationship with our personal God. However you choose to spend your time with him, try to allow time for praise, prayer, and reading of Scripture. *Reflections* are provided at the end of each session for you to use as part of your daily time with God. These will offer reinforcement of the principles you are learning, and develop or strengthen your habit of time alone with God throughout the week.

19. Before you close your group in prayer, answer this question: "How can we pray for you this week?" Write prayer requests on your *Prayer and Praise Report* and commit to praying for each other throughout the week.

Study Notes

Tree of the Knowledge of Good and Evil: This tree signifies the giving of knowledge of good and evil. Stealing this knowledge leads to spiritual, and eventually physical, death. The knowledge referred to is moral knowledge (discernment). God created Adam and Eve with a degree of moral discernment, the ability to know obedience from disobedience. But they don't understand evil either as a concept or from experience. In eating from the tree, they disobey God and so understand evil from personal experience.

If Adam had not disobeyed God, God might eventually have let him come to understand evil by observing it in other creatures like Satan. In fact, Adam might have understood evil more deeply that way, without experiencing it. One doesn't need to be a drug addict in order to understand addiction, and addicts can be in denial about things in themselves that are obvious to non-addicts who closely observe them. So God wasn't trying to keep Adam from growing up. He was trying to help Adam grow up in good time, in the right way.

It was not therefore a "power" imbued by the tree that gave Adam knowledge of evil, but the act of disobedience that gave it.

The Fall: This term is used to describe the rebellious state of humanity, which occurred when Adam and Eve willfully disobeyed God and ate from the tree of knowledge of good and evil. The Bible makes it clear that every person is a sinner before he or she has opportunity to sin because the capacity to sin is inborn, inherited from Adam and Eve as a result of the Fall.

Seed of the Woman: The offspring of the woman who would eventually crush the serpent's (Satan's) head is Jesus Christ.

The Curse: A term used to describe God's judgments on creation after the Fall.

For Deeper Study (Optional)

Read Romans 5:12–21 and answer the questions below.

1. What do verses 12–14 suggest about the effect that Adam's sin had on humanity?

2. Contrast the gift of God through Jesus Christ with the judgment of God through Adam as stated in verses 16–19.

3. Romans 5:17 tells us that death reigned as a result of sin. Notice that verse 21 says sin reigned in death. As death reigned over our lives, sin reigned as well. What does this suggest about the nature of man resulting from the Fall? What does verse 21 say is accomplished through Jesus Christ?

4. Romans 5:15–21 provides a clear contrast between the condemning act of Adam and the redeeming act of Jesus Christ. How does this passage bring clarity to your understanding of God's promise to restore his relationship to humanity through Jesus Christ?

Reflections

Reading, reflecting, and meditating on the Word of God is essential to getting to know him deeply. As you read the verses each day, give prayerful consideration to what you learn about God, his Spirit, and his place in your life. Then record your thoughts, insights, or prayer in the *Reflect* section below the verses you read. On the sixth day, record a summary of what you learned over the entire week through this study.

Day 1. So God created man in his own image, in the image of God he created him; male and female he created them (Gen. 1:27 NIV).

REFLECT

_____

_____

_____

_____

Day 2. Consequently, just as the result of one trespass was condemnation for all men, so also the result of one act of righteousness was justification that brings life for all men. For just as through the disobedience of the one man the many were made sinners, so also through the obedience of the one man the many will be made righteous (Rom. 5:18–19 NIV).

REFLECT

_____

_____

_____

_____

Day 3. For the wages of sin is death, but the gift of God is eternal life in Christ Jesus our Lord (Rom. 6:23 NIV).

REFLECT

_____

_____

_____

_____

Day 4. He is the image of the invisible God, the firstborn over all creation. For by Him all things were created that are in heaven and that are on earth, visible and invisible, whether thrones or dominions or principalities or powers. All things were created through Him and for Him. And He is before all things, and in Him all things consist (Col. 1:15–17 NKJV).

REFLECT

_____

_____

_____

_____

Day 5. For all have sinned and fall short of the glory of God (Rom. 3:23 NIV).

REFLECT

_____

_____

_____

_____

Day 6. Use the following space to write any insight God has put in your heart and mind about the things we have looked at in this session and during your *Reflections* time this week.

SUMMARY

_____

_____

_____

_____

THE PROMISE DEMONSTRATED
THE ABRAHAMIC COVENANT

Memory Verse: No longer will you be called Abram; your name will be Abraham, for I have made you a father of many nations (Gen. 17:5 NIV).

According to the *American Heritage Dictionary*, promise means to make a declaration assuring that something will or will not be done. Notice that this definition does not say to have good intentions of following through. Too often people make promises, or assurances, that are really better defined as good intentions. We want to do this or that, but when push comes to shove, we just don't deliver. It is no surprise people are skeptical to trust our word.

We may not be able to trust one another to keep promises all the time, but Scripture assures us that God not only has good intentions; when he promises that something will or will not be done, it is accomplished according to his Word. God's promise is one we can count on.

 **Connecting**

Open your group with prayer, inviting the Holy Spirit to remove any uncertainty that you may have in God's faithfulness to keep his promises.

1. If you have new people joining you for the first time, take a few minutes to briefly introduce yourselves.

2. Healthy small groups *rotate leadership*. We recommend that you rotate leaders on a regular basis. This practice helps to develop every member's ability to shepherd a few people within a safe environment. Even Jesus gave others the opportunity to serve alongside him (Mark 6:30–44).

   It's also a good idea to *rotate host homes*, with the host of each meeting providing the refreshments. Some groups like to let the host lead the meeting, while others like to allow one person host while another person leads.

   The *Small Group Calendar* is a tool for planning who will lead and host each meeting. Take a few minutes to plan leaders and hosts for your remaining meetings. Don't pass this up! It will revolutionize your group.

   For information on leading your assigned study session, see the *Leader's Notes* introduction and notes for the session you will be leading. You can find these in the *Appendix*. Also, if you are leading for the first time, see *Leading for the First Time (Leadership 101)* in the *Appendix*. If you still have questions refer to the *Frequently Asked Questions (FAQs)* in the *Appendix*.

3. Share a time when you experienced a promise, either fulfilled or unfulfilled, that affected your expectations about future promises.

 **Growing**

In the garden of Eden, God promised to restore his relationship with humanity through the offspring, or "seed," of Eve (Gen. 3:15). In Genesis 12:1–9 we find God's acting on that promise of blessing through his call of Abram (whose name God later changes to Abraham) to become the father of many nations.
Read Genesis 12:1–9 aloud.

4. Look at the command God gives to Abram in 12:1. What costs and risks do you think obeying such a command involved in the ancient world? See the *Study Notes* for help.

5. Abraham is faced with the choice to obey God or not, with very little hard information. How is he like or unlike Adam in the choice he faces, the decision he makes, and the consequences?

6. Notice the aspects of God's promise to Abraham (12:2–3) identified below. How are the promises significant for Abraham? For humankind?

Aspects of God's Promise to Abraham (Gen. 12:2–3 NIV)	Significance for Abraham	Significance for Humankind
I will make you into a great nation and I will bless you;		
I will make your name great, and you will be a blessing.		
I will bless those who bless you, and whoever curses you I will curse;		

26

Aspects of God's Promise to Abraham (Gen. 12:2–3 NIV)	Significance for Abraham	Significance for Humankind
All peoples on earth will be blessed through you.		

7. What do the following verses reveal about how Jesus, Abraham's greatest son, is the fulfillment of God's promise to Abraham?

☐ Matthew 1:1

☐ Luke 1:54–55, 71–75

☐ Luke 19:1–10

☐ Acts 3:13–15

☐ Romans 4:13–16

☐ Galatians 3:6–9, 14

8. How does it matter to you personally that Jesus fulfilled the promise to Abraham? (Look back at Gen. 12:2–3 and think about how you have experienced the fulfillment of this promise.)

9. As promised, God made Abraham's name great. Jews, Muslims, and Christians revere his name as a model of faith. According to Hebrews 11:8–12, 17–19, how is Abraham a model of faith that includes obedience?

10. What opportunities for acting in obedient faith do you have today?

God extended the promise he initiated in Genesis 3:15 when he called Abraham to leave his home country to go to a land that God would show him. Abraham trusted God and was faithful to obey, so God gave him the blessings God had promised. God's faithfulness to Abraham offered hope that God would eventually fulfill his ultimate promise—the restoration of his people to right relationship with him.

Developing

Accountability means being answerable for our actions. Spiritual accountability happens when we invite someone into our lives for the purpose of encouraging our faith journeys and challenging one another in specific areas of desired growth. Hebrews 3:12–13 says: "See to it, brothers, that none of you has a sinful, unbelieving heart that turns away from the living God. But encourage one another daily, as long as it is called Today, so that none of you may be hardened by sin's deceitfulness" (NIV). Opening our lives to someone and making ourselves vulnerable to their loving admonition could perhaps be one of the most difficult things to do; however, it could also result in the deepest and most lasting spiritual growth we've known.

11. Scripture tells us in Ephesians 4:25–26: "Laying aside falsehood, speak truth, each one of you with his neighbor, for we are members of one another" (NASB). With this in mind, take a moment to pair up with someone in your group to be your spiritual partner for the remainder of this study. We strongly recommend men partner with men, and women with women. (Refer to the *Leader's Notes* for this question in the *Appendix* for information on what it means to be a spiritual partner.)

    Turn to the *Personal Health Plan* in the Appendix. In the box that says, "WHO are you connecting with spiritually?" write your partner's name.

    In the box that says, "WHAT is your next step for growth?" write one step you would like to take for growth during this study. Tell your partner what step you chose. When you check in with your partner each meeting, the "Partner's Progress" column on this chart will provide a place to record your partner's progress in the goal he or she chose.

12. Spending time together outside of group meetings helps to build stronger relationships within your group as you get to

28

know each other better. Discuss whether your group would like to have a potluck or other type of social to celebrate together what God is doing in your group. You could plan to share a meal prior to a small group meeting or plan to follow your completion of this study with a meal together—maybe a barbecue. Appoint one or two people who can follow up with everyone outside of group time to put a plan together.

Sharing

During the past week you should have been thinking about the people in your life with whom you come into regular contact. These make up your circles of influence or *Circles of Life*.

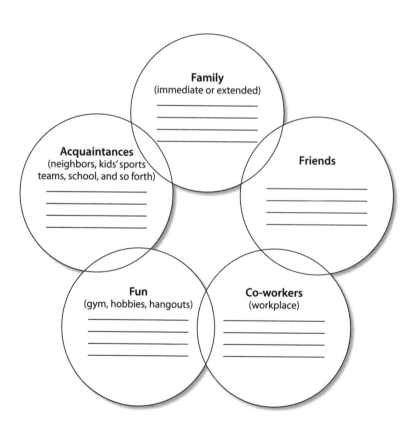

13. Take a look at the *Circles of Life* diagram (previous page) and think of people you know in each category who need to be connected in Christian community. Write the names of two or three people in each circle.

The people who fill these circles are not there by accident. God has strategically placed each of them within your sphere of influence because he has equipped you to minister to them and share with them in ways no one else can. Consider the following ideas for reaching out to one or two of the people you listed and make a plan to follow through with them this week.

☐ This is a wonderful time to welcome a few friends into your group. Which of the people you listed could you invite? It's possible that you may need to help your friend overcome obstacles to coming to a place where he or she can encounter Jesus. Does your friend need a ride to the group or help with childcare?

☐ Consider inviting a friend to attend a weekend church service with you and possibly plan to enjoy a meal together afterward. This can be a great opportunity to talk with someone about your faith in Jesus.

☐ Is there someone who is unable to attend your group or church but who still needs a connection? Would you be willing to have lunch or coffee with that person, catch up on life, and share something you've learned from this study? Jesus doesn't call all of us to lead small groups, but he does call every disciple to spiritually multiply his or her life over time.

 Surrendering

In a world where promises are often just forgotten good intentions, it's hard to believe that anyone is faithful to keep them, but David assures us in Psalm 145:13b: "The LORD is faithful to all his promises and loving toward all he has made" (NIV). If not for the faithfulness of the Lord our God to honor his Word, we would still be living

30

hopeless lives, destined to spend eternity separated from our awesome creator.

14. Take a few minutes to talk about what it would take to make time with God a priority every day or even five or six days a week. Don't put time demands on yourself at first; just make it a priority to draw near to God for a few minutes each day and gradually you will desire more. Use the *Reflections* at the end of each session as a starting point.

15. Share your prayer requests as a group. Be sure to record everyone's requests on your *Prayer and Praise Report*. Use these as reminders to pray for everyone throughout the week.

Study Notes

The Call of Abram (Abraham): God told Abram to leave his country and people and go. Such a command was highly countercultural, since clan and family were the source of a person's strength and protection. God was asking Abram to leave his known territory, tight-knit community, and family to go somewhere about which he knew nothing.

For Deeper Study (Optional)

God's promise to Abraham is stated in Genesis 12:1, but actually is woven all the way through chapter 22. Look at the sevenfold structure of God's promise to Abraham as stated in Genesis 12:2–3:

- I will make you into a great nation
- I will bless you
- I will make your name great

31

- You will be a blessing
- I will bless those who bless you
- Whoever curses you I will curse
- All peoples on earth will be blessed through you

Read the following verses and identify which of the seven aspects of God's promise you see God beginning to fulfill.

- Genesis 12:10–20
- Genesis 13:2
- Genesis 13:14–17
- Genesis 14:11–24
- Genesis 15:1–6
- Genesis 15:12–16

Continue reading through chapter 22 of the book of Genesis. Pay special attention to events or words of God that continue to show Abraham his faithfulness to fulfill his promise. Why do you think that God didn't fulfill his promise immediately? What benefits are gained by waiting?

Reflections

Hopefully last week you made a commitment to read, reflect, and meditate on the Word of God each day. Following are selections of Scripture provided as a starting point to drawing near to God through time with him. Read the daily verses and then record your thoughts, insights, or prayers in the space provided. On the sixth day, record a summary of what you have learned over the entire week through this study or use this space to write down how God has challenged you personally.

Day 1. By faith Abraham, when called to go to a place he would later receive as his inheritance, obeyed and went, even though he did not know where he was going. By faith he made his home in the promised land like a stranger in a foreign country; he lived in tents, as did Isaac and Jacob, who were heirs with him of the same promise. For he was looking forward to the city with foundations, whose architect and builder is God (Heb. 11:8–10 NIV).

REFLECT

_____

_____

_____

_____

Day 2. Against all hope, Abraham in hope believed and so became the father of many nations, just as it had been said to him, "So shall your offspring be." Without weakening in his faith, he faced the fact that his body was as good as dead—since he was about a hundred years old—and that Sarah's womb was also dead. Yet he did not waver through unbelief regarding the promise of God, but was strengthened in his faith and gave glory to God, being fully persuaded that God had power to do what he had promised (Rom. 4:18–21 NIV).

REFLECT

_____

_____

_____

_____

Day 3. Consider Abraham: "He believed God, and it was credited to him as righteousness." Understand, then, that those who believe are children of Abraham. The Scripture foresaw that God would justify the Gentiles by faith, and announced the gospel in advance to Abraham: "All nations will be blessed through you." So those who have faith are blessed along with Abraham, the man of faith (Gal. 3:6–9 NIV).

REFLECT

_____

_____

_____

_____

Day 4. Now I am about to go the way of all the earth. You know with all your heart and soul that not one of all the good promises the LORD your God gave you has failed. Every promise has been fulfilled; not one has failed (Josh. 23:14 NIV).

REFLECT

_____

_____

_____

_____

Day 5. Since we have these promises, dear friends, let us purify ourselves from everything that contaminates body and spirit, perfecting holiness out of reverence for God (2 Cor. 7:1 NIV).

REFLECT

_____

_____

_____

_____

Day 6. Use this space to record insights, thoughts, or prayers that God has given you during *Session Two* and your *Reflections* time.

SUMMARY

_____

_____

_____

_____

THE PROMISE INDIVIDUALIZED
THE DAVIDIC COVENANT

Memory Verse: One day as these men were worshiping the Lord and fasting, the Holy Spirit said, "Dedicate Barnabas and Saul for the special work I have for them" (Acts 13:2 NLT).

When J. Hudson Taylor was just three years old, he made the bold prediction that he would become a missionary to China. He could not have known then how it would come to pass, or even that it would. But as Taylor grew into a faith-filled man, his prediction became reality in spite of many obstacles and apparent failings. He founded China Inland Mission in 1865 that served China and the Lord Jesus Christ for almost 100 years.

When God promised Adam and Eve that he would someday restore fellowship between humanity and God, he not only knew that it would come to pass, but he knew the details that would come together to make it a reality. He knew that Abraham would be a man full of faith and obedience to his call. He knew that Abraham would become the father of many nations even while his wife Sarah had been barren for ninety-nine years. And he knew that the Messiah would reign forever on David's throne. God doesn't make bold predictions with hope that they come true; he makes promises that we can depend on.

Connecting

Begin your group discussion time by praying Psalm 86:11 which says: "Teach me your way, O LORD, and I will walk in your truth; give me an undivided heart, that I may fear your name" (NIV).

1. Most people want to live a healthy, balanced life. A regular medical check-up is a good way to measure health and spot potential problems. In the same way, a spiritual check-up is vital to your spiritual well-being. The *Personal Health Assessment* was designed to give you a quick snapshot, or pulse, of your spiritual health.

   Take a few minutes alone to complete the *Personal Health Assessment* in the *Appendix*. After answering each question, tally your results. Then, pair up with your spiritual partner and briefly share one purpose that is going well and one that needs a little work. Then go to the *Personal Health Plan* in the *Appendix* and record one next step you plan to take in the area of the purpose you want to work on. If you haven't established your spiritual partnership yet, do it now. (Refer to the *Session Two, Leader's Notes, Developing* section in the *Appendix* for help.)

2. When have you made a hopeful prediction that something would transpire for you or someone you know? Share what happened.

Growing

The promise God made to Abraham was passed down to his son Isaac, then to Isaac's son Jacob/Israel, and then to the twelve tribes who descended from Israel. The promise focused on one of the twelve tribes, Judah, and then was traced through the line of one of Judah's descendants, King David. God promised David that through him God would raise up a king, the Messiah, who would reign on his throne forever.

3. Recall from Genesis 12:2–3 that God promised Abraham to make from him a great nation and to bless all nations through him. In Genesis 26:24, God makes a promise to Abraham's son Isaac. How does this verse show that Isaac has inherited his father's promise?

4. Isaac's son Jacob/Israel has twelve sons, and from them descend the twelve tribes of Israel. In Genesis 49 we see Jacob blessing his sons, prophesying not only their personal futures but also the futures of their descendants.

Genesis 49:8–12 records Jacob's blessing to his son Judah. What do these verses indicate about God's plan for Judah's descendants? (See the *Study Notes* for information about the scepter.)

5. Read Matthew 1:1–6. What is said here about Abraham, Jacob, Judah, and King David?

6. David lived about eight hundred years after Judah. Read 1 Samuel 16:1–13. Here the prophet Samuel anoints David with oil to declare him king of Israel (kings in Israel were anointed rather than crowned). What's the connection between this event and the promise Judah received in Genesis 49:10?

7. Read 2 Samuel 7:1–17. What does God promise to King David?

How are these promises connected to what was promised to Judah?

How are these promises connected to what God promised Abraham?

8. In 2 Samuel 7:16, God promises David that he will raise up a descendant ("seed") after him who will reign on David's throne forever. Read Isaiah 9:1–7. What does this prophecy say about the king who will reign on David's throne?

9. This expected king camed to be called the Messiah, which means "anointed one," because kings in Israel were anointed. If you knew nothing more about this king than what you've read so far in the Old Testament, would you expect him to be a political leader of an earthly kingdom? Explain.

10. Centuries later, Jesus lived and was killed. The apostle Peter saw him alive again, and in Acts 2:22–36 we see Peter claiming that Jesus is the Messiah, the promised descendant of David. What evidence does Peter give for believing that Jesus is the Messiah?

How are Peter's statements in 2:33 significant for us?

11. How does it matter to us that this promise was handed down over the centuries and fulfilled in Jesus?

God's promise continues to unfold as it passes from Abraham through the tribe of Judah to King David, through whom the Messiah comes to reign forever.

Developing

God created each of us to serve him within the body of Christ. None of us can "opt out" of this service because, just as our physical body needs all of its parts to function and thrive, the spiritual body of Christ needs all of its parts as well. It is because of the vast number of needs represented by the countless people and circumstances around us that he has given every believer unique gifts. Each of us has something very special to offer to fill specific needs within the church.

12. Discuss some of the many ways that we can serve the body of Christ. Is there a particular area of service that God has put

on your heart to serve either this group or in your local church? If not, investigate the opportunities and pray about finding a ministry in which you can serve. As you take that first step, God will lead you to the ministry that expresses your passion.

13. On your *Personal Health Plan*, in the "Develop" section, answer the "WHERE are you serving?" question. If you are not currently serving, note one area where you will consider serving.

Sharing

All around us, people are struggling to find purpose for life, often looking to prestige, possessions, and people to fill the void in their life that only God can fill. In Matthew 5:14–16 Jesus says, "You are the light of the world. A city on a hill cannot be hidden. Neither do people light a lamp and put it under a bowl. Instead they put it on its stand, and it gives light to everyone in the house. In the same way, let your light shine before men, that they may see your good deeds and praise your Father in heaven" (NIV). A godly example can be a beacon of hope, shining light into a person's dark circumstances. You can become a visible reminder of God's design for others as you seek to live out his purposes in your life.

14. In the last session you were asked to write some names in the *Circles of Life* diagram. Go back to the *Circles of Life* diagram to remind yourself of the various people you come into contact with on a regular basis. Have you followed up with those you identified who need to connect with other Christians? If not, when will you contact them?

Surrendering

Praise is focusing our hearts on God. Psalm 149:1 says: "Praise the Lord. Sing to the LORD a new song, his praise in the assembly of the saints" (NIV). It's important that we take a moment to prepare our hearts to enter into the presence of God by praising him through prayer.

15. Share your praises and prayer requests with one another. Record these on the *Prayer and Praise Report*. Then, pair up with your spiritual partner and spend time praying for each other. Then, come back together in one group and someone close the group time in prayer.

Study Notes

Scepter: A wand or a rod that the king holds as a sign of his royal power and authority.

For Deeper Study (Optional)

Read 2 Samuel 7:8–16. What similarities exist between God's promise given to David and his promise given to Abraham as we studied in *Session Two?*

1. How do these relate to God's promise stated in Genesis 3:15?

2. How does God say he will fulfill his promise to David from this passage?

3. Even though God's promise here has immediate fulfillment in David's son Solomon, it has a greater fulfillment in Jesus. In your own words, describe how this promise relates to the eventual coming and reign of the Messiah.

4. Read 1 Chronicles 22:7–10. What did David say happened that prevented him from building the house for the Lord in 1 Chronicles 22:8? What did God promise to do instead?

5. What does God's promise through Solomon in spite of David's failings teach us about the nature of God's promises? How does this provide believers today with hope in God's promises to us?

Reflections

If you've been committed to spending time each day connecting with God through his Word, congratulations! Some experts say that it takes 21 repetitions to develop a new habit. By the end of this week, you'll be well on your way to cultivating new spiritual habits that will encourage you in your walk with God. This week, continue to read the daily verses, giving prayerful consideration to what you learn about God, his Spirit, and his place in your life. Then, as before, record your thoughts, insights, or prayers in the space provided. On the sixth day, record a summary of what you have learned throughout the week.

Day 1. He remembers his covenant forever, the word he commanded, for a thousand generations, the covenant he made with Abraham, the oath he swore to Isaac. He confirmed it to Jacob as a decree, to Israel as an everlasting covenant (Ps. 105:8–10 NIV).

REFLECT

_____

_____

_____

_____

Day 2. I will sing of the LORD's great love forever; with my mouth I will make your faithfulness known through all generations. I will declare that your love stands firm forever, that you established your faithfulness in heaven itself. You said, "I have made a covenant with my chosen one, I have sworn to David my servant, 'I will establish your line forever and make your throne firm through all generations'" (Ps. 89:1–4 NIV).

REFLECT

Day 3. He chose David his servant and took him from the sheep pens; from tending the sheep he brought him to be the shepherd of his people Jacob, of Israel his inheritance (Ps. 78:70–71 NIV).

REFLECT

Day 4. The promises were spoken to Abraham and to his seed. The Scripture does not say "and to seeds," meaning many people, but "and to your seed," meaning one person, who is Christ (Gal. 3:16 NIV).

REFLECT

Day 5. But the angel said to her, "Do not be afraid, Mary, you have found favor with God. You will be with child and give birth to a son, and you are to give him the name Jesus. He will be great and will be called the Son of the Most High. The Lord God will give him the throne of his father David, and he will reign over the house of Jacob forever; his kingdom will never end" (Luke 1:30–33 NIV).

REFLECT

_____

_____

_____

_____

Day 6. Record your weekly summary of what God has shown you in the space below.

SUMMARY

_____

_____

_____

_____

THE PROMISE INCARNATED

THE ARRIVAL OF THE MESSIAH

Memory Verse: For to us a child is born, to us a son is given, and the government will be on his shoulders. And he will be called Wonderful Counselor, Mighty God, Everlasting Father, Prince of Peace. Of the increase of his government and peace there will be no end. He will reign on David's throne and over his kingdom, establishing and upholding it with justice and righteousness from that time on and forever. The zeal of the Lord Almighty will accomplish this (Isa. 9:6–7 NIV).

In Acts 12 Peter was imprisoned, held in chains and guarded by four squads of four soldiers. While he was in prison, there was a group of believers who were vehemently praying for his release. The Bible tells us that during the night an angel of the Lord appeared, released Peter's chains and led him safely out of the prison. He arrived shortly after at the door of Mary's house where the believers had been praying. That night, the believers experienced the faithfulness of God to answer prayer.

Throughout ancient history, religious leaders and scholars have prayed in anticipation of the coming of God's promised Messiah. In *Session Four* of our study of the *Promises of God*, the fulfillment of God's promise is realized through the arrival of his Son, Jesus

Christ. God is not only faithful to answer prayer; he is faithful to keep his promises.

Connecting

Open your group with words of praise for what God has given you through his promised Son, Jesus Christ. Thank him for what he has shown you during the last few weeks of your study of the *Promises of God*, and ask him to open the eyes of your heart that you might know him even better in the coming weeks.

1. Take five minutes to check in with your spiritual partner, or with another partner if yours is absent. Share with your partner how your time with God went this week. What is one thing you discovered? Or, what obstacles hindered you from following through? Turn to your *Personal Health Plan*. Make a note about your partner's progress and how you can pray for him or her.

2. Think of a time when you waited a very long time for something. What did you wait for, and how did you feel when it finally happened?

Growing

In *Session Three* we saw God's faithfulness in keeping the promise he made in the garden of Eden, continued with Abraham, and individualized to the lineage of King David. We saw that Jesus is *the* descendant of David who will reign on David's throne forever. Today we'll look at how God made promises through prophets about the Messiah (King) and how Jesus fulfilled them.

3. Compare these Old Testament prophecies to their New Testament fulfillments. In each case, how does Jesus fulfill the prophecy?

Old Testament Prophecy	New Testament Fulfillment
Isaiah 7:14	Luke 1:26–38
Micah 5:2	Luke 2:1–7
Hosea 11:1	Matthew 2:13–15

What do you think we're meant to learn from seeing these fleeting comments from the Old Testament prophets fulfilled in Jesus's birth?

4. According to Isaiah 11:1–2; 42:1; 61:1–2, how is the Messiah prepared for ministry?

How does Jesus fulfill these prophecies (Luke 3:21–22; 4:14–21)?

Why do you suppose the Holy Spirit's role needed to be emphasized like this?

5. Look again at Isaiah 61:1–2, as well as Isaiah 35:5–10. How do these passages help to explain why Jesus spent so much time healing the sick and disabled, and addressing the needs of the poor?

What does it say about God and his kingdom that these are the signs by which the King is known? (You might think about how God might have done things differently, perhaps by sending a Savior who would have killed all the corrupt Jews and cruel Romans in Palestine.)

6. Many expected God to fulfill his promise to set the oppressed free (Luke 4:18; Isa. 61:1) through a conquering king that would deliver them from Rome's oppressive rule. But God had much greater plans. He sent a King who brings justice and hope to

all nations by conquering sin and death. Which do you value more: freedom from sin and death, or political and personal freedom? Please explain.

7. Have you ever expected God to answer your prayers in a specific way, but later saw that he did something better but unexpected? If so, describe that experience.

8. Before Jesus's ministry went public, God prepared him for what was to come. Luke 4:1–13 tells us how the Holy Spirit led Jesus into the wilderness, where Satan tempted him. Read this passage and compare it to Genesis 3:1–15. How do you think these two incidents are linked?

9. During his forty-day temptation in the wilderness, Jesus quoted three times from Deuteronomy (Deut. 8:3; 6:13,16; see Luke 4:8–12). In this part of Deuteronomy, Moses explains the lessons the Israelites should have learned from forty years in the wilderness, between their liberation from Egypt and their entrance into the Promised Land. Why do you suppose Jesus deliberately relived the lessons Israel was supposed to learn, but didn't?

10. In his earthly life and ministry, Jesus fulfilled much more of the Old Testament than we have time to cover here. What value is there to us in understanding how the whole Old Testament points forward to Christ?

Through his birth and public ministry, Jesus fulfilled the Old Testament prophecies concerning the Messiah and set God's plan of redemption in motion. See *Study Notes* to help you better understand Jesus as the fulfillment of the prophecies we've studied in this session.

Developing

First Peter 4:10–11 says: "Each one should use whatever gift he has received to serve others, faithfully administering God's grace in its various forms" (NIV). Last session we talked about using our God-given gifts to serve him in the body of Christ. Today we will spend some time exploring the gifts we are given.

11. The Bible lists the many spiritual gifts given to believers. Take five minutes and review the *Spiritual Gifts Inventory* in the *Appendix*. Discuss which of the listed gifts you believe you may have. If you are unsure, you can review the inventory with a trusted friend who knows you well. Chances are they have witnessed one or more of these gifts in your life.

    Once you have an idea about what your spiritual gifts may be, discuss how you may be able to use them in ministry. Plan to investigate the opportunities available to you in your church and get involved in serving the body of Christ. It's amazing to experience God using you to fill a specific need within his church.

Sharing

Acts 4:31 says: "After they prayed, the place where they were meeting was shaken. And they were all filled with the Holy Spirit and spoke the word of God boldly" (NIV). God empowers us through his Holy Spirit to share Jesus boldly and without hindrance.

12. In *Session Two*, you identified people within your *Circles of Life* that needed connection to Christian community. Jesus's commission in Acts 1:8 included sharing him not only within our own circles of influence (our Jerusalem), but also in Judea and Samaria and the ends of the earth. Judea included the region in which Jerusalem was located. Today, this might include neighboring communities or cities. As a group, discuss the following possible actions you can take to share Jesus with your Judea in a tangible way.

    ☐ Collect new blankets and/or socks for the homeless. Bring them with you next week and have someone deliver them to a ministry serving the homeless.

48

☐ Bring nonperishable food items to the next group meeting and designate one person to donate them to a local food bank.

☐ As a group, pick a night to volunteer to serve meals at a mission or homeless shelter.

13. On your *Personal Health Plan,* in the "Sharing" section, answer the "WHEN are you shepherding another person in Christ?" question.

Surrendering

First John 3:11 says: "This is the message you heard from the beginning: We should love one another" (NIV). One way to show our love for one another is to pray focused prayer over each other's needs.

Study Notes

Old Testament Prophecies: The Old Testament prophecies we cover in this session and in *Session Five* are described as "fulfilled" by Jesus in the New Testament, but not all of them are uniquely fulfilled by him. In other words, some have an original Old Testament context that is not exclusively about Jesus. Jesus fulfills these "typologically" in the sense that he is the culmination of God's plan of salvation. Hosea 11:1 is a good example. It was originally about Israel's exodus from Egypt, but Matthew applies it to Jesus to show that Jesus is taking into himself and reliving the whole history of Israel. Just as God brought his "son" Israel out of Egypt and expected them to be a light of revelation to the Gentiles (Isa. 42:6; 49:6), so Jesus, the true Son of God, is the true Israel who comes out of Egypt and brings light to the Gentiles. Jesus is what Israel should have been.

Other prophecies, such as Micah's prediction about the Messiah's birth in Bethlehem, are uniquely fulfilled in Jesus. For us today, these fulfillments give us assurance that God keeps his promises. Scripture is reliable for us to stand on.

For Deeper Study (Optional)

Over 300 prophecies in the Bible speak of Jesus Christ. Read the following verses and reflect on Jesus's fulfillment of these prophecies that were written, in some cases, thousands of years before his birth and ministry.

- Genesis 22:8
- Psalm 89:26–29
- Isaiah 22:21–25
- Isaiah 25:8
- Daniel 7:13–14
- Daniel 9:24

1. How do each of these prophecies foretell of Jesus?

2. What confidence do these fulfilled prophecies give you in God's faithfulness?

3. Listed below are just a few additional Messianic prophecies.
   ☐ Deuteronomy 18:15–19
   ☐ 2 Samuel 23:2–4
   ☐ Psalm 22
   ☐ Psalm 69
   ☐ Isaiah 9:6–7

Reflections

Second Timothy 3:16–17 reads: "All Scripture is God-breathed and is useful for teaching, rebuking, correcting and training in righteousness, so that the man of God may be thoroughly equipped for every good work" (NIV). Allow God's Word to train you in righteousness as you read, reflect on, and respond to the Scripture in your daily time with God this week.

Day 1. For to us a child is born, to us a son is given, and the government will be on his shoulders. And he will be called Wonderful Counselor, Mighty God, Everlasting Father, Prince of Peace. Of the increase of his government and peace there will be no end. He will reign on David's throne and over his kingdom, establishing and upholding it with justice and righteousness from that time on and forever. The zeal of the LORD Almighty will accomplish this (Isa. 9:6–7 NIV).

REFLECT

_____

_____

_____

_____

Day 2. A voice of one calling: "In the desert prepare the way for the LORD; make straight in the wilderness a highway for our God. Every valley shall be raised up, every mountain and hill made low; the rough ground shall become level, the rugged places a plain. And the glory of the LORD will be revealed, and all mankind together will see it. For the mouth of the LORD has spoken" (Isa. 40:3–5 NIV).

REFLECT

_____

_____

_____

_____

Day 3. The Spirit of the LORD will rest on him—the Spirit of wisdom and of understanding, the Spirit of counsel and of power, the Spirit of knowledge and of the fear of the LORD—and he will delight in the fear of the LORD (Isa. 11:2–3 NIV).

REFLECT

_____

_____

_____

_____

Day 4. Behold! My Servant whom I uphold, My Elect One in whom My soul delights! I have put My Spirit upon Him; He will bring forth justice to the Gentiles (Isa. 42:1 NKJV).

REFLECT

_____

_____

_____

_____

Day 5. Then will the eyes of the blind be opened and the ears of the deaf unstopped. Then will the lame leap like a deer, and the mute tongue shout for joy. Water will gush forth in the wilderness and streams in the desert (Isa. 35:5–6 NIV).

REFLECT

_____

_____

_____

_____

Day 6. Use the following space to record your summary of how God has challenged you this week.

SUMMARY

_____

_____

_____

_____

THE PROMISE FULFILLED

THE DEATH AND RESURRECTION OF THE MESSIAH

Memory Verse: Therefore I will give him a portion among the great, and he will divide the spoils with the strong, because he poured out his life unto death, and was numbered with the transgressors. For he bore the sin of many, and made intercession for the transgressors (Isa. 53:12 NIV).

In Luke 15, Jesus tells the story of a man who had two sons. The younger son asked for his share of his father's inheritance and left for a distant land where he squandered his money and was forced to make a living feeding pigs, the ultimate indignity for a Jew. Realizing he had hit rock bottom, he decided to return home in hopes of becoming a servant in his father's house. The father had long been watchfully waiting with anticipation for the return of his son. When he saw him coming from far off, he ran to him with open arms, accepting him fully into his household with all the rights due a son. Luke 15:32 sums up the father's heart best saying: "We had to celebrate and be glad, because this brother of yours was dead and is alive again; he was lost and is found" (NIV).

Our heavenly Father had been long waiting for his reunion with humanity. From the time of Adam and Eve's original sin to the resurrection of our Lord, he had been anticipating the day that we would return home and assume our rightful place as members of his household. And just like the father of the prodigal son, there is much celebration as we who were once dead, become alive again through the fulfillment of his promise, Jesus Christ.

Connecting

Psalm 100:4 says: "Enter his gates with thanksgiving and his courts with praise; give thanks to him and praise his name" (NIV). As you begin your time together, offer a prayer of thanksgiving for all that God has done so far in your small group. Ask him to open your heart to receive his message for you today.

1. Check in with your spiritual partner, or with another partner if yours is absent. Talk about any challenges you are currently facing in reaching the goals you have set throughout this study. Tell your spiritual partner how he or she has helped you follow through with each step. Be sure to write down your partner's progress.

2. Share a time when you or someone you know has experienced joy over a long overdue reunion with a friend or loved one.

Growing

In this session we will see that the promise of Genesis 3:15, woven through the lives of Abraham and his descendents, reaches fulfillment through the death and resurrection of the Messiah. A great many Old Testament passages point toward his death and resurrection, but we will focus closely on just one.

Read Isaiah 52:13–53:12. This is one of several passages in which Isaiah foresees someone whom God calls "my servant."

3. How does Isaiah describe the servant's appearance (52:14; 53:2)?

How does Jesus fulfill this? (You might look at Matthew 27:26–44.)

4. How do you see Isaiah's words in 53:3 fulfilled in Matthew 27:26–44?

Isaiah calls the servant "despised" and "familiar with suffering" (53:3). Do you think these things were true of Jesus before he was arrested? Please explain.

5. How does Isaiah 53:4–5 help us understand what Jesus was doing on the cross?

6. Isaiah predicts that the servant will keep his mouth shut when led to the slaughter (53:7). Look at Matthew 27:11–14. Why do you suppose Jesus refuses to answer the charges when he is interrogated?

7. Compare Isaiah 53:9 to Matthew 27:57–60. How does Matthew's account echo Isaiah's?

8. Isaiah clearly says in 53:9 that the servant will die and be buried. Yet in 53:10–11 he says the servant will see his offspring, and will see the light of life and be satisfied. Verse 12 ends the passage on a note of triumph and exaltation. How does Jesus fulfill this promise?

How is it important to us that Jesus was not abandoned to the grave?

9. In Jesus's day, the Jewish people did not commonly expect that the Messiah (the descendant of David who would reign on his throne) and Isaiah's suffering servant would be the same person. Put Isaiah 9:1–7 and 52:13–53:12 side by side. Why

might it have been hard for even Jesus's disciples to see these two prophecies as pointing to the same person?

10. How do these two passages, side by side, explain who Jesus is and what he has done?

11. Go back to Genesis 3:15. How does Jesus, the suffering servant, fulfill this promise? (You might look at Heb. 2:14–15.)

12. How does it matter to us that Jesus fulfilled centuries-old predictions in both his death and his resurrection?

The life, ministry, death, and resurrection of the Messiah fulfilled Scripture and accomplished our salvation by paying the penalty of death for our sins. Not only can we be confident in this, but, because of the fulfillment of God's Genesis 3:15 promise, we can be convinced that our God keeps all of his promises to us.

Developing

During the previous four weeks, hopefully you've developed some new growth disciplines such as accountability, Scripture memorization, meditation on the Word of God, and daily time with God. Consider taking your commitment to know God better one step further this week.

13. If you've been spending time each day in personal focused prayer, doing *Reflections*, and/or meditating on God's Word, consider taking your commitment a step further this week by journaling. Read through *Journaling 101* found in the *Appendix*. Commit this week to spending a portion of your time with God journaling.

14. During *Session Two*, you should have discussed whether your group would like to have a potluck or social. Take a few minutes now to tie up any loose ends in your plan.

15. Briefly discuss the future of your group. How many of you are willing to stay together as a group and work through another study? If you have time, turn to the *Small Group Agreement* and talk about any changes you would like to make as you move forward as a group.

Sharing

In *Session One*, we talked about Jesus's final command to his disciples in Acts 1:8: "Be my witnesses in Jerusalem, and in all Judea and Samaria, and to the ends of the earth" (NIV). Jesus wanted his disciples to share his gospel not only with their local communities, but also the world. *You* can be involved in taking the gospel to *all* nations.

16. In previous sessions you were asked to identify people who need to be connected in Christian community. Return to the *Circles of Life* diagram. Outside each circle, write down one or two names of people you know who need to know Christ. Commit to praying for an opportunity to share Jesus with each of them. You may invite them to attend an outreach event with you or you may feel led to share the good news with him or her over coffee. Share your commitment with your spiritual partner. Pray together for God's Holy Spirit to give you the words to speak with boldness.

17. Prayerfully consider the following actions as a first step toward fulfilling Jesus's commission in your life.

    ☐ Hang a world map in the place where you pray at home. Pray for the world, then each continent, and then each country as the Lord leads you; or pray for the countries printed on your clothing labels as you get dressed every day.

    ☐ Send financial support to a missionary in a foreign country or a world mission organization. Your church will likely have suggestions for who this might be.

☐ Sponsor a child through a Christ-centered humanitarian aid organization.

Surrendering

Philippians 4:6 tells us: "Do not be anxious about anything, but in everything, by prayer and petition, with thanksgiving, present your requests to God" (NIV). Prayer represents a powerful act of surrender to the Lord as we put aside our pride and lay our burdens at his feet.

18. Share prayer requests and spend some time praying for them.

19. Spend a moment silently praying as David did in Psalm 139:23–24, "Search me, O God, and know my heart; test me and know my anxious thoughts. See if there is any offensive way in me, and lead me in the way everlasting" (NIV).

For Deeper Study (Optional)

1. Atonement is the act by which God restores the relationship of humanity with himself. Read Leviticus 17:11 and Hebrews 9:22. According to these verses, why is the shedding of blood required for atonement?

2. Redemption is deliverance from the penalty of sin by paying a price. Jesus's death accomplished this for us by his atoning sacrifice on our behalf. According to Romans 3:23–25 and 6:23, why is death necessary in order to be redeemed?

3. According to Hebrews 10:8–10, why do you think God required sacrifices and offerings if he was not pleased with them? What effect then, did Jesus's death have on this established system for atonement?

4. Colossians 1:21–23 touches on the point that through Jesus's death we became reconciled to God. In what condition are we presented to God? How does this relate to the condition from which mankind fell as a result of Adam and Eve's sin?

Reflections

The Lord promised Joshua success and prosperity in Joshua 1:8 when he said: "Do not let this Book of the Law depart from your mouth; meditate on it day and night, so that you may be careful to do everything written in it. Then you will be prosperous and successful" (NIV). We too can claim this promise for our lives as we commit to meditate on the Word of God each day. As in previous weeks, read and meditate on the daily verses and record any insights you gain in the space provided. Summarize what you have learned this week on Day 6.

Day 1. The disciples went and did as Jesus had instructed them. They brought the donkey and the colt, placed their cloaks on them, and Jesus sat on them. A very large crowd spread their cloaks on the road, while others cut branches from the trees and spread them on the road. The crowds that went ahead of him and those that followed shouted, "Hosanna to the Son of David!" "Blessed is he who comes in the name of the Lord!" "Hosanna in the highest!" When Jesus entered Jerusalem, the whole city was stirred and asked, "Who is this?" The crowds answered, "This is Jesus, the prophet from Nazareth in Galilee" (Matt. 21:6–11 NIV).

REFLECT

_____

_____

_____

_____

Day 2. The stone the builders rejected has become the capstone; the LORD has done this, and it is marvelous in our eyes. This is the day the LORD has made; let us rejoice and be glad in it (Ps. 118:22–24 NIV).

REFLECT

_____

_____

_____

_____

Day 3. Therefore I will give him a portion among the great, and he will divide the spoils with the strong, because he poured out his life unto death, and was numbered with the transgressors. For he bore the sin of many, and made intercession for the transgressors (Isa. 53:12 NIV).

REFLECT

_____

_____

_____

_____

Day 4. Later, knowing that all was now completed, and so that the Scripture would be fulfilled, Jesus said, "I am thirsty." A jar of wine vinegar was there, so they soaked a sponge in it, put the sponge on a stalk of the hyssop plant, and lifted it to Jesus' lips. When he had received the drink, Jesus said, "It is finished." With that, he bowed his head and gave up his spirit (John 19:28–30 NIV).

REFLECT

_____

_____

_____

_____

Day 5. After the Sabbath, at dawn on the first day of the week, Mary Magdalene and the other Mary went to look at the tomb. There was a violent earthquake, for an angel of the Lord came down from heaven and, going to the tomb, rolled back the stone and sat on it. His appearance was like lightning, and his clothes were white as snow. The guards were so afraid of him that they shook and became like dead men. The angel said to the women, "Do not be afraid, for I know that you are looking for Jesus, who was crucified. He is not here; he has risen, just as he said. Come and see the place where he lay. Then go quickly and tell his disciples: 'He has risen from the dead and is going ahead of you into Galilee. There you will see him.' Now I have told you" (Matt. 28:1–7 NIV).

REFLECT

_____

_____

_____

_____

Day 6. Use the following space to write any thoughts God has put in your heart and mind during *Session Five* and your *Reflections* time this week.

SUMMARY

_____

_____

_____

_____

THE PROMISE REALIZED IN BELIEVERS
THE PRESENCE OF GOD'S SPIRIT

Memory Verse: You, however, are controlled not by the sinful nature but by the Spirit, if the Spirit of God lives in you. And if anyone does not have the Spirit of Christ, he does not belong to Christ (Rom. 8:9 NIV).

The Grand Coulee Dam, located on the Columbia River in Eastern Washington, is the largest hydroelectric power producer in North America and the third largest in the world. Because of its awesome display, it might be easy to assume that the power is generated by the thousands of gallons of water pouring over the 1,650-foot spillway, but the reality is the power comes from the hidden turbines and generators that lie deep within the enormous concrete structure.

Just as the power of the Grand Coulee Dam resides deep within its core, the power of the Holy Spirit indwells the heart of every believer. The power that indwells believers lies within us transforming our lives from the inside out, renewing our spirit, guiding our daily lives, empowering our ministry, and convicting our souls.

Connecting

Begin this session with prayer in the spirit of David reflected in Psalm 19:14: "May the words of my mouth and the meditation of my heart be pleasing in your sight, O LORD, my Rock and my Redeemer" (NIV).

1. Check in with your spiritual partner. Share your progress on the goals you set for yourself during this study and share any challenges you are currently facing.

   Take a few minutes to pray for each other now. Be sure to write down your partner's progress.

2. Have you ever experienced transformation? If so, when? (Try to keep your answer to a few sentences, as you'll have more to say about this later.)

Growing

The promise of the Messiah in Genesis 3:15 offers hope for humanity's reconciliation with God. This promise becomes personal for all believers as God fufills the prophetic words of Isaiah and Joel by pouring the Holy Spirit into our lives.

3. Isaiah predicted that the anointed King would have not just ordinary oil but the Holy Spirit poured on him. Go back to Isaiah 61:1–2 and note some of the things the Holy Spirit empowers the Messiah to do.

4. What does the prophet Joel foresee in Joel 2:28–32?

   In these verses, what effect does the Holy Spirit have on people?

5. In Acts 1:1–9, Jesus has risen from the dead, has spent forty days teaching his disciples, and is now visiting them physically for the last time. From now on he will be with his Father, and his disciples won't see him. What does he say about the Holy

Spirit in this passage? (See the *Study Note* on "Baptized with [or in] the Spirit.")

Why will the disciples need the Spirit?

6. Acts 2:1–21 describes what happens ten days later, on the Jewish feast of Pentecost. How are Jesus's and Joel's words fulfilled here?

What impression of the Holy Spirit and his work do you get from the imagery of wind (v. 2) and fire (v. 3)?

7. Why do you suppose some onlookers think the disciples are drunk (Acts 2:13)?

8. What might be the significance of this happening to "all people . . . sons and daughters . . . young men . . . old men . . . both men and women" (Acts 2:17–18)?

9. Why do you suppose God pours out the Spirit so dramatically in this situation?

10. As described in Isaiah, Joel, and Acts, how would you summarize what the Holy Spirit does?

The Holy Spirit does a great deal more than this, and you could spend several weeks studying what he does. He gives believers new birth into a new life (John 3:5–6). He teaches and guides us into truth (John 14:26; 15:26; 16:12–15). He (not we) convicts the world of sin (John 16:8–11). Much of that is far less outwardly dramatic than what Joel and Acts describe.

Underlying most of these diverse works of the Spirit is this: The Holy Spirit *transforms* people. He changes them. He gives them abilities they didn't have. He gives them truth they didn't have. He uproots vices and instills virtues.

11. How does Paul describe the Spirit's work of transformation in 2 Corinthians 3:17–18?

12. Have you experienced the Spirit's work of transformation? If so, how?

13. Is transformation by the Holy Spirit something you want? Please explain.

The fulfillment of the Old Testament promise in the life of believers comes through the transforming work of the Holy Spirit, who is the presence of God in our lives.

Developing

Jesus modeled self-sacrificing service as he washed his disciples' feet in the upper room just before his arrest. He humbled himself to perform the menial task usually reserved for the lowliest of servants. In John 13:15, he instructed his disciples to follow his example saying: "I have set you an example that you should do as I have done for you" (NIV). Jesus's words should compel us to serve, but his example should inspire us to serve with hearts of humility and a willingness to get our hands dirty.

14. To serve as Jesus did, we need to be willing to humble ourselves to carry out even the most menial of tasks. This could mean doing yard work, painting a house, or cleaning for someone who is in need. Discuss how you might serve a needy family in your church. Devise a game plan and then commit to seeing it through. You could choose one or two people who are willing to follow up with your church or a local ministry to put your plan into action.

Sharing

Today we talked about the role of the Holy Spirit in sharing spiritual truths with unbelievers. We also learned that as believers filled with the Holy Spirit, we are given power to share the message of Christ boldly.

15. Telling your own story is a powerful way to share Jesus with others. Turn to *Telling Your Story* in the *Appendix*. Review this with your spiritual partner. Begin developing your story by taking a few minutes to share briefly what your life was like before you knew Christ. (If you haven't yet committed your life to Christ or became a Christian at a very young age and don't remember what life was like before Christ, reflect on what you have seen in the life of someone close to you.) Make notes about this aspect of your story below and commit to writing it out this week. Then, spend some time individually developing your complete story using the *Telling Your Story* exercise in the *Appendix*.

_____

_____

_____

16. In this study we have seen Jesus as the fulfillment of the Old Testament prophecies concerning the Messiah, God's anointed Savior. If you have never invited Jesus to take control of your life, why not ask him now? If you are not clear about God's gift of eternal life for everyone who believes in Jesus and how to receive this gift, take a minute to pray and ask God to help you understand what he wants you to do about trusting in Jesus.

 ## Surrendering

Scripture tells us in Proverbs 15:29: "The LORD . . . hears the prayer of the righteous" (NIV).

17. Turn to the *Personal Health Plan* and individually consider the "HOW are you surrendering your heart?" question. Look to the *Sample Personal Health Plan* for help. Share some of your thoughts with the group.

18. Look back over the *Prayer and Praise Report*. Are there any answered prayers? Spend a few minutes sharing these in simple, one-sentence prayers of thanks to God. It's important to share

your praises along with prayer requests each week so you can see where God is working in your lives.

Share any new prayer requests you have with the group and record them on the *Prayer and Praise Report*.

Study Notes

The great and dreadful day of the Lord: One of the challenging things we face as we read the Old Testament prophets is that God didn't show the prophets a time gap between the Messiah's first and second comings. So in Joel 2:28–32, for example, "the great and dreadful day of the LORD" seems to be one simultaneous event. The Spirit is poured out and there are signs in the heavens—so much smoke in the air that the sun goes dark and the moon turns blood-red. From our vantage point, it seems that some of what Joel describes was fulfilled two thousand years ago at Pentecost, while other things he describes sound like Revelation, Christ's second coming. Both Christ's first and second comings (and the time in between) can be described as "the day of the Lord."

Baptized with [or in] the Holy Spirit: The meaning of this phrase is much disputed, but the Greek suggests that metaphorically the Spirit is like a liquid—a person can be immersed into the Spirit, or the Spirit can be poured onto a person. Of course, the Spirit isn't literally a liquid any more than he is literally wind or fire. These are images by which the biblical writers try to help us get a sense of what receiving the Spirit is like. The Spirit isn't an impersonal thing or force, he is a Person.

For Deeper Study (Optional)

Read Romans 8:1–27. Identify the work of the Holy Spirit found in the following selected verses:

- Verses 2–3:
- Verse 4:
- Verses 5–7:
- Verses 10–13:
- Verses 14–16:
- Verses 17–18:
- Verses 22–27:

Read Galatians 5:16–26, which contrasts living according to the sinful nature to living by the Spirit.

1. What attitudes characterize each life?

2. To what are those without the Holy Spirit bound? How does one live a life led by the Spirit according to verse 24?

Reflections

Get into harmony with God as you spend time with him this week. Read and reflect on the daily verses. Then record your thoughts, insights, or prayers in the *Reflect* sections that follow. On the sixth day record your summary of what God has taught you this week.

Day 1. God has raised this Jesus to life, and we are all witnesses of the fact. Exalted to the right hand of God, he has received from the Father the promised Holy Spirit and has poured out what you now see and hear (Acts 2:32–33 NIV).

REFLECT

_____

_____

_____

_____

Day 2. And afterward, I will pour out my Spirit on all people. Your sons and daughters will prophesy, your old men will dream dreams, your young men will see visions (Joel 2:28 NIV).

REFLECT

_____

_____

_____

_____

Day 3. The Spirit of the Sovereign LORD is on me, because the LORD has anointed me to preach good news to the poor. He has sent me to bind up the brokenhearted, to proclaim freedom for the captives and release from darkness for the prisoners, to proclaim the year of the LORD's favor and the day of vengeance of our God, to comfort all who mourn, and provide for those who grieve in Zion—to bestow on them a crown of beauty instead of ashes, the oil of gladness instead of mourning, and a garment of praise instead of a spirit of despair. They will be called oaks of righteousness, a planting of the LORD for the display of his splendor (Isa. 61:1–3 NIV).

REFLECT

_____

_____

_____

_____

Day 4. Jesus answered, "I tell you the truth, no one can enter the kingdom of God unless he is born of water and the Spirit. Flesh gives birth to flesh, but the Spirit gives birth to spirit. You should not be surprised at my saying, 'You must be born again.' The wind blows wherever it pleases. You hear its sound, but you cannot tell where it comes from or where it is going. So it is with everyone born of the Spirit" (John 3:5–8 NIV).

REFLECT

_____

_____

_____

_____

Day 5. And you also were included in Christ when you heard the word of truth, the gospel of your salvation. Having believed, you were marked in him with a seal, the promised Holy Spirit, who is a deposit guaranteeing our inheritance until the redemption of those who are God's possession—to the praise of his glory (Eph. 1:13–14 NIV).

REFLECT

_____

_____

_____

_____

Day 6. Record your summary of what God has taught you this week.

SUMMARY

_____

_____

_____

_____

THE PROMISE FINALIZED

Memory Verse: And even we Christians, although we have the Holy Spirit within us as a foretaste of future glory, also groan to be released from pain and suffering. We, too, wait anxiously for that day when God will give us our full rights as his children, including the new bodies he has promised us (Rom. 8:23 NLT).

Our culture strives for perfection when it comes to outward appearances. The television, Internet, and print media are all teeming with advertisements and articles about how to turn back the clock. Most of us, in varying degrees, want to smooth away wrinkles, shed extra pounds and have more energy.

Scripture holds good news for those of us who long for better bodies. God has promised to release us from our aging, failing bodies. We do, however have to wait patiently as Romans 8:24–25 says: "Now that we are saved, we eagerly look forward to this freedom . . . . But if we look forward to something we don't have yet, we must wait patiently and confidently" (NLT).

In the culmination of God's promise to Adam and Eve in Genesis 3:15, we will trade in the perishable bodies in which we now live for the new, perfect, imperishable bodies that he intended from the beginning. And with those new bodies, we will finally receive *our full rights as his adopted children* (Rom. 8:23 NLT).

Connecting

Begin this final session with prayer. Thank God for how he has challenged and encouraged you during this study.

1. This is the last time to connect with your spiritual partner in your small group. What has God been showing you through these sessions about his faithfulness? Have you gained a more full trust in his ability to keep his promises? Check in with each other about the progress you have made in your spiritual growth during this study. Plan whether you will continue in your mentoring relationship outside your Bible study group.

2. Share with the group one thing you have learned about God and his promises during this study that has encouraged you. Also, if you have questions as a result of this study, discuss where you might find the answers.

Growing

In this session we look at the culmination of the Genesis 3:15 promise about the restoration of all things. We have explored much of what God has done over many centuries to provide the way for this fulfillment.

Read 1 Corinthians 15:1–11.

3. What does the apostle Paul say in 15:1–11 to assure us that Christ's resurrection actually happened?

Paul writes 1 Corinthians about 25 years after Jesus's resurrection, when many of the eyewitnesses are still alive. He has personally met some of them, and he is an eyewitness himself. On what basis would we believe or disbelieve him and them?

Read 1 Corinthians 15:12–34.

4. According to 15:20–22, why is the resurrection of Christ significant to the fulfillment of Genesis 3:15?

   See the *Study Notes* on "in Adam" and "in Christ." What does it mean for you to be "in Christ"?

5. Why does Paul say that if Christ wasn't really raised bodily from the dead, then we Christians are to be pitied (15:17–19)?

6. In 15:23–28 Paul describes what will happen when Christ returns to earth a second time. According to verse 23, what's the first thing that will happen?

   What will happen after that?

7. How do our natural bodies compare to our glorified bodies according to 1 Corinthians 15:35–53?

8. Our natural bodies are weak and perishable, but our glorified bodies will be powerful and no longer perishable. What does 1 Corinthians 15:54–58 say we can expect about sickness, suffering, and death when we receive our new body?

9. How does Paul's idea of bodily resurrection differ from being an immortal soul in some spiritual place?

10. How is resurrection different from reincarnation?

11. When Christ returns, how does 15:50–54 paint the picture of what will happen to believers who have died before his return?

    What will happen to those who are still alive?

12. What difference does your hope of eventually rising from the dead make to your life now?

In a dramatic culmination of God's promise in Genesis 3:15, the resurrection of Christ reversed the effects of Adam's fall. His resurrection was the firstfruit of our final resurrection. It guarantees that we too will be raised. Our resurrection will put an end to death. We will receive our immortal, imperishable, glorified bodies at the second coming of Christ, when God will create a new heaven and a new earth (Rom. 8:18–25; Rev. 21–22). This will be the final restoration to all of creation. Just as God was faithful to keep his original promise, we can count on his faithfulness to keep his promises today.

Developing

Ezekiel 3:3 says: "'Son of man, eat this scroll I am giving you and fill your stomach with it.' So I ate it, and it tasted as sweet as honey in my mouth" (NIV). This week as we wrap up our study of the *Promises of God*, recommit to spending regular time eating God's scroll, the Bible. Don't just give it a casual glance or rush to get through a Bible reading plan, but really chew it up, digest it and allow every word to nourish you. Not only will you find that it strengthens your faith and assurance of God's promises, but as it's absorbed deep into your hearts, you will find it sweetens your life.

13. If time permits, one or two of you share how a new discipline started in this study has transformed your relationship with God.

14. If your group still needs to make decisions about continuing to meet after this session, have that discussion now. Talk about what you will study, who will lead, and where and when you will meet.

    Review your *Small Group Agreement* and evaluate how well you achieved your goals. Discuss any changes you want to make as you move forward. As your group starts a new study this is a great time to take on a new role or change roles of service in your group. What new role will you take on? If you are uncertain, maybe your group members have some ideas for you. Remember you aren't making a lifetime commitment to the new role; it will only be for a few weeks. Maybe someone would like to share a role with you if you don't feel ready to serve solo.

Sharing

Scripture tells us that we should always be prepared to give an answer for the hope that we have found in Christ. That's what sharing Christ is all about.

15. During the course of this seven-week study, you have made many commitments to share Jesus with the people in your life, either in inviting your believing friends to grow in Christian community or by sharing the gospel in words or actions with unbelievers. Share with the group any highlights that you have experienced as you've stepped out in faith to share with others.

Surrendering

16. Close by sharing and praying for your prayer requests and take a couple of minutes to review the praises you have recorded over the past few weeks on the *Prayer and Praise Report*. Thank God for what he's done in your group during this study.

Study Notes

In Adam/In Christ: We can think of these as two regimes. We humans are far more connected to one another than most of us in the modern world are aware of. We are born connected to Adam; Adam is the head of humanity. What Adam did affects us all, and that's why we die. But by shifting our allegiance to Christ, we become "in Christ" instead of "in Adam." We are now connected to Christ, and he is the head of a new humanity. In most of Paul's letters he goes to great effort to convince us to think of ourselves as "in Christ" and to act accordingly.

For Deeper Study (Optional)

Acts 3:21 says: "He must remain in heaven until the time comes for God to restore everything, as he promised long ago through his holy prophets" (NIV). God has destined his entire creation for restoration and renewal. The prophet Isaiah recorded the Word of the Lord: "Behold, I will create new heavens and a new earth. The former things will not be remembered, nor will they come to mind" (Isa. 65:17 NIV).

1. Read and reflect on Revelation 21:1–5. How does it make you feel to know that someday you'll live on the new earth where there will be no more death, mourning, crying, or pain?

2. How does Revelation 22:1–5 describe our restored relationship with God? Which aspect of this description is most significant to you?

Reflections

As you read through this final week of *Reflections*, prayerfully consider what God is showing you about his character, the Holy Spirit, and how he wants you to grow and change. Then, write down your thoughts or prayers in the space provided. Don't let this concluding week that you spend doing *Reflections* be the last. Commit to continue reading, reflecting, and meditating on the Word of God daily. Use Day 6 to record your prayer of commitment to see this discipline become habit.

Day 1. But Christ has indeed been raised from the dead, the first-fruits of those who have fallen asleep. For since death came through a man, the resurrection of the dead comes also through a man. For as in Adam all die, so in Christ all will be made alive (1 Cor. 15:20–22 NIV).

REFLECT

_____

_____

_____

_____

Day 2. The creation waits in eager expectation for the sons of God to be revealed. For the creation was subjected to frustration, not by its own choice, but by the will of the one who subjected it, in hope that the creation itself will be liberated from its bondage to decay and brought into the glorious freedom of the children of God (Rom. 8:19–21 NIV).

REFLECT

_____

_____

_____

_____

Day 3. We know that the whole creation has been groaning as in the pains of childbirth right up to the present time. Not only so, but we ourselves, who have the firstfruits of the Spirit, groan inwardly as we wait eagerly for our adoption as sons, the redemption of our bodies (Rom. 8:22–23 NIV).

REFLECT

_____

_____

_____

_____

Day 4. So will it be with the resurrection of the dead. The body that is sown is perishable, it is raised imperishable; it is sown in dishonor, it is raised in glory; it is sown in weakness, it is raised in power; it is sown a natural body, it is raised a spiritual body (1 Cor. 15:42–44 NIV).

REFLECT

_____

_____

_____

_____

Day 5. So it is written: "The first man Adam became a living being"; the last Adam, a life-giving spirit. The spiritual did not come first, but the natural, and after that the spiritual. The first man was of the dust of the earth, the second man from heaven. As was the earthly man, so are those who are of the earth; and as is the man from heaven, so also are those who are of heaven. And just as we have borne the likeness of the earthly man, so shall we bear the likeness of the man from heaven (1 Cor. 15:45–49 NIV).

REFLECT

_____

_____

_____

_____

Day 6. Use the following space to write out your prayer of commitment to continue spending daily time with God in his Word and prayer.

SUMMARY

_____

_____

_____

_____

FREQUENTLY ASKED QUESTIONS

What do we do on the first night of our group?

Like all fun things in life—have a party! A "get to know you" coffee, dinner, or dessert is a great way to launch a new study. You may want to review the *Small Group Agreement* and share the names of a few friends you can invite to join you. But most importantly, have fun before your study time begins.

Where do we find new members for our group?

This can be challenging, especially for new groups that have only a few people or for existing groups that lose a few people along the way. We encourage you to pray with your group and then brainstorm a list of people from work, church, your neighborhood, your children's school, family, the gym, and so forth. Then have each group member invite several of the people on his or her list. Another good strategy is to ask church leaders to make an announcement that your group is open to new members.

No matter how you find members, it's vital that you stay on the lookout for new people to join your group. All groups tend to go through healthy attrition—the result of moves, releasing new leaders, ministry opportunities, and so forth—and if the group gets too small, it could be at risk of shutting down. If you and your group stay open, you'll be amazed at the people God sends your way. The next person just might become a friend for life. You never know!

How long will this group meet?

It's totally up to the group—once you come to the end of this study. Most groups meet weekly for at least their first six months together, but every other week can work as well. We strongly recommend that the group meet for the first six months on a weekly basis if at all possible. This allows for continuity, and if people miss a meeting they aren't gone for a whole month.

At the end of this study, each group member may decide whether he or she wants to continue on for another study. Some groups launch relationships that last for years, and others are stepping-stones into another group experience. Either way, enjoy the journey.

What if this group is not working for me?

Personality conflicts, life stage differences, geographical distance, level of spiritual maturity, or any number of things can cause you to feel the group doesn't work for you. Relax. Pray for God's direction, and at the end of this study decide whether to continue with this group or find another. You don't buy the first car you look at or marry the first person you date, and the same goes with a group. Don't bail out before the study is finished—God might have something to teach you. Also, don't run from conflict or prejudge people before you have given them a chance. God is still working in you too!

Who is the leader?

Most groups have an official leader. But ideally, the group will mature and members will share the facilitation of meetings. We have discovered that healthy groups share hosting and leading of the group. This model ensures that all members grow, give their unique contribution, and develop their gifts. This study guide and the Holy Spirit can keep things on track even when you share leadership. Christ has promised to be in your midst as you gather. Ultimately, God is your leader each step of the way.

How do we handle the child care needs in our group?

This can be a sensitive issue. We suggest that you empower the group to openly brainstorm solutions. You may try one option that works for a while and then adjust over time. Our favorite approach is for adults to meet in the living room or dining room, and share the cost of a babysitter (or two) who can be with the kids in a different part of the house. In this way, parents don't have to be away from their children all evening when their children are too young to be left at home. A second option is to use one home for the kids and a second home (close by) for the adults. A third idea is to rotate the responsibility of providing a lesson or care for the children either in the same home or in another home nearby. This can be an incredible blessing for kids. Finally, the most common idea is to decide that you need to have a night to invest in your spiritual lives individually or as a couple, and make your own arrangements for child care. No matter what decision the group makes, the best approach is to dialogue openly about both the problem and the solution.

SMALL GROUP AGREEMENT

Our Purpose

To transform our spiritual lives by cultivating our spiritual health in a healthy small group community. In addition, we:

_____

_____

_____

Our Values

Group Attendance	To give priority to the group meeting. We will call or e-mail if we will be late or absent. (Completing the *Small Group Calendar* will minimize this issue.)
Safe Environment	To help create a safe place where people can be heard and feel loved. (Please, no quick answers, snap judgments, or simple fixes.)
Respect Differences	To be gentle and gracious to people with different spiritual maturity, personal opinions, temperaments, or imperfections. We are all works in progress.
Confidentiality	To keep anything that is shared strictly confidential and within the group, and avoid sharing improper information about those outside the group.
Encouragement for Growth	To be not just takers but givers of life. We want to spiritually multiply our lives by serving others with our God-given gifts.

Welcome for Newcomers	To keep an open chair and share Jesus's dream of finding a shepherd for every sheep.
Shared Ownership	To remember that every member is a minister and to ensure that each attender will share a small team role or responsibility over time. (See the *Team Roles*.)
Rotating Hosts/ Leaders and Homes	To encourage different people to host the group in their homes, and to rotate the responsibility of facilitating each meeting. (See the *Small Group Calendar*.)

Our Expectations

- Refreshments/mealtimes _____
- Child care _____
- When we will meet (day of week) _____
- Where we will meet (place) _____
- We will begin at (time) _____ and end at _____
- We will do our best to have some or all of us attend a worship service together. Our primary worship service time will be _____
- Date of this agreement _____
- Date we will review this agreement again _____
- Who (other than the leader) will review this agreement at the end of this study _____

TEAM ROLES

The Bible makes clear that every member, not just the small group leader, is a minister in the body of Christ. In a healthy small group, every member takes on some small role or responsibility. It can be more fun and effective if you team up on these roles.

Review the team roles and responsibilities below, and have each member volunteer for a role or participate on a team. If someone doesn't know where to serve or is holding back, as a group, suggest a team or role. It's best to have one or two people on each team so you have each of the five purposes covered. Serving in even a small capacity will not only help your leader but also will make the group more fun for everyone. Don't hold back. Join a team!

The opportunities below are broken down by the five purposes and then by a *crawl* (beginning), *walk* (intermediate), or *run* (advanced) role. Try to cover at least the crawl and walk roles, and select a role that matches your group, your gifts, and your maturity.

Team Roles	Team Player(s)

CONNECTING TEAM (Fellowship and Community Building)

Crawl: Host a social event or group activity in the first week or two. _____

Walk: Create a list of uncommitted friends and then invite them to an open house or group social. _____

Run: Plan a twenty-four-hour retreat or weekend getaway for the group. Lead the *Connecting* time each week for the group. _____

GROWING TEAM (Discipleship and Spiritual Growth)

Crawl: Coordinate the spiritual partners for the group. Facilitate a three- or four-person discussion circle during the Bible study portion of your meeting. Coordinate the discussion circles. _____

Walk: Tabulate the *Personal Health Plans* in a summary to let people know how you're doing as a group. Encourage personal devotions through group discussions and pairing up with spiritual (accountability) partners. _____

Run: Take the group on a prayer walk, or plan a day of solitude, fasting, or personal retreat. _____

SERVING TEAM (Discovering Your God-Given Design for Ministry)

Crawl: Ensure that every member finds a group role or team he or she enjoys. _____

Walk: Have every member take a gift test and determine your group's gifts. Plan a ministry project together. _____

Run: Help each member decide on a way to use his or her unique gifts somewhere in the church. _____

SHARING TEAM (Sharing and Evangelism)

Crawl: Coordinate the group's *Prayer and Praise Report* of friends and family who don't know Christ. _____

Walk: Search for group mission opportunities and plan a cross-cultural group activity. _____

Run: Take a small group "vacation" to host a six-week group in your neighborhood or office. Then come back together with your current group. _____

SURRENDERING TEAM (Surrendering Your Heart to Worship)

Crawl: Maintain the group's *Prayer and Praise Report* or journal. _____

Walk: Lead a brief time of worship each week (at the beginning or end of your meeting). _____

Run: Plan a more unique time of worship. _____

SMALL GROUP CALENDAR

Planning and calendaring can help ensure the greatest participation at every meeting. At the end of each meeting, review this calendar. Be sure to include a regular rotation of host homes and leaders, and don't forget birthdays, socials, church events, holidays, and mission/ministry projects.

Date	Lesson	Dessert/Meal	Role

PERSONAL HEALTH ASSESSMENT

	Just Beginning	Getting Going	Well Developed

CONNECTING with God's Family

I am deepening my understanding of and friendship with God in community with others. — 1 2 3 4 5

I am growing in my ability both to share and to show my love to others. — 1 2 3 4 5

I am willing to share my real needs for prayer and support from others. — 1 2 3 4 5

I am resolving conflict constructively and am willing to forgive others. — 1 2 3 4 5

CONNECTING Total _____

GROWING to Be Like Christ

I have a growing relationship with God through regular time in the Bible and in prayer (spiritual habits). — 1 2 3 4 5

I am experiencing more of the characteristics of Jesus Christ (love, patience, gentleness, courage, self-control, etc.) in my life. — 1 2 3 4 5

I am avoiding addictive behaviors (food, television, busyness, and the like) to meet my needs. — 1 2 3 4 5

I am spending time with a Christian friend (spiritual partner) who celebrates and challenges my spiritual growth. — 1 2 3 4 5

GROWING Total _____

89

	Just Beginning	Getting Going	Well Developed

DEVELOPING Your Gifts to Serve Others

I have discovered and am further developing my unique God-given design. — 1 2 3 4 5

I am regularly praying for God to show me opportunities to serve him and others. — 1 2 3 4 5

I am serving in a regular (once a month or more) ministry in the church or community. — 1 2 3 4 5

I am a team player in my small group by sharing some group role or responsibility. — 1 2 3 4 5

DEVELOPING Total _____

SHARING Your Life Mission Every Day

I am cultivating relationships with non-Christians and praying for God to give me natural opportunities to share his love. — 1 2 3 4 5

I am praying and learning about where God can use me and our group cross-culturally for missions. — 1 2 3 4 5

I am investing my time in another person or group who needs to know Christ. — 1 2 3 4 5

I am regularly inviting unchurched or unconnected friends to my church or small group. — 1 2 3 4 5

SHARING Total _____

SURRENDERING Your Life for God's Pleasure

I am experiencing more of the presence and power of God in my everyday life. — 1 2 3 4 5

I am faithfully attending services and my small group to worship God. — 1 2 3 4 5

I am seeking to please God by surrendering every area of my life (health, decisions, finances, relationships, future, etc.) to him. — 1 2 3 4 5

I am accepting the things I cannot change and becoming increasingly grateful for the life I've been given. — 1 2 3 4 5

SURRENDERING Total _____

Personal Health Assessment

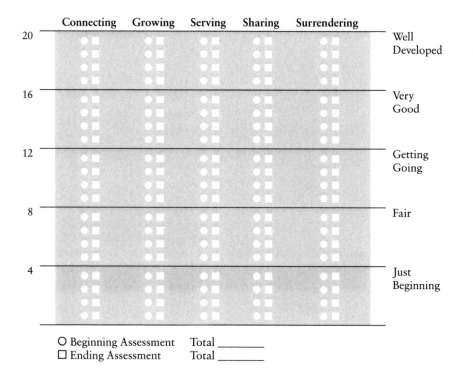

O Beginning Assessment   Total _____
□ Ending Assessment   Total _____

PERSONAL HEALTH PLAN

This worksheet could become your single most important feature in this study. On it you can record your personal priorities before the Father. It will help you live a healthy spiritual life, balancing all five of God's purposes.

PURPOSE	PLAN
CONNECT	WHO are you connecting with spiritually?
GROW	WHAT is your next step for growth?
DEVELOP	WHERE are you serving?
SHARE	WHEN are you shepherding another in Christ?
SURRENDER	HOW are you surrendering your heart to God?

DATE	MY PROGRESS	PARTNER'S PROGRESS

Personal Health Plan

DATE	MY PROGRESS	PARTNER'S PROGRESS

SAMPLE PERSONAL HEALTH PLAN

This worksheet could become your single most important feature in this study. On it you can record your personal priorities before the Father. It will help you live a healthy spiritual life, balancing all five of God's purposes.

PURPOSE	PLAN
CONNECT	WHO are you connecting with spiritually?
	Bill and I will meet weekly by e-mail or phone
GROW	WHAT is your next step for growth?
	Regular devotions or journaling my prayers 2×/week
DEVELOP	WHERE are you serving?
	Serving in children's ministry Go through GIFTS Assessment
SHARE	WHEN are you shepherding another in Christ?
	Shepherding Bill at lunch or hosting a starter group in the fall
SURRENDER	HOW are you surrendering your heart?
	Help with our teenager New job situation

DATE	MY PROGRESS	PARTNER'S PROGRESS
3/5	Talked during our group	Figured out our goals together
3/12	Missed our time together	Missed our time together
3/26	Met for coffee and review of my goals	Met for coffee
4/10	E-mailed prayer requests	Bill sent me his prayer requests
5/5	Great start on personal journaling	Read Mark 1–6 in one sitting!
5/12	Traveled and not doing well this week	Journaled about Christ as healer
5/26	Back on track	Busy and distracted; asked for prayer
6/1	Need to call Children's Pastor	
6/26	Group did a serving project together	Agreed to lead group worship
6/30	Regularly rotating leadership	Led group worship–great job!
7/5	Called Jim to see if he's open to joining our group	Wanted to invite somebody, but didn't
7/12	Preparing to start a group in fall	
7/30	Group prayed for me	Told friend something I'm learning about Christ
8/5	Overwhelmed but encouraged	Scared to lead worship
8/15	Felt heard and more settled	Issue with wife
8/30	Read book on teens	Glad he took on his fear

SPIRITUAL GIFTS INVENTORY

A spiritual gift is given to each of us as a means of helping the entire church.

1 Corinthians 12:7 (NLT)

A spiritual gift is a special ability, given by the Holy Spirit to every believer at their conversion. Although spiritual gifts are given when the Holy Spirit enters new believers, their use and purpose need to be understood and developed as we grow spiritually. A spiritual gift is much like a muscle; the more you use it, the stronger it becomes.

A Few Truths about Spiritual Gifts

1. Only believers have spiritual gifts. 1 Corinthians 2:14
2. You can't earn or work for a spiritual gift. Ephesians 4:7
3. The Holy Spirit decides what gifts I get. 1 Corinthians 12:11
4. I am to develop the gifts God gives me. Romans 11:29; 2 Timothy 1:6
5. It's a sin to waste the gifts God gave me. 1 Corinthians 4:1–2; Matthew 25:14–30
6. Using my gifts honors God and expands me. John 15:8

Gifts Inventory

God wants us to know what spiritual gift(s) he has given us. One person can have many gifts. The goal is to find the areas in which the Holy Spirit seems to have supernaturally empowered our service to others. These gifts are to be used to minister to others and build up the body of Christ.

There are four main lists of gifts found in the Bible in Romans 12:3–8; 1 Corinthians 12:1–11, 27–31; Ephesians 4:11–12; and 1 Peter 4:9–11. There are other passages that mention or illustrate gifts not included in these lists. As you read through this list, prayerfully consider whether the biblical definition describes you. Remember, you can have more than one gift, but everyone has at least one.

ADMINISTRATION (Organization)—1 Corinthians 12
This is the ability to recognize the gifts of others and recruit them to a ministry. It is the ability to organize and manage people, resources, and time for effective ministry.

APOSTLE—1 Corinthians 12
This is the ability to start new churches/ventures and oversee their development.

DISCERNMENT—1 Corinthians 12
This is the ability to distinguish between the spirit of truth and the spirit of error; to detect inconsistencies in another's life and confront in love.

ENCOURAGEMENT (Exhortation)—Romans 12
This is the ability to motivate God's people to apply and act on biblical principles, especially when they are discouraged or wavering in their faith. It is also the ability to bring out the best in others and challenge them to develop their potential.

EVANGELISM—Ephesians 4
This is the ability to communicate the gospel of Jesus Christ to unbelievers in a positive, nonthreatening way and to sense opportunities to share Christ and lead people to respond with faith.

FAITH—1 Corinthians 12

This is the ability to trust God for what cannot be seen and to act on God's promise, regardless of what the circumstances indicate. This includes a willingness to risk failure in pursuit of a God-given vision, expecting God to handle the obstacles.

GIVING—Romans 12

This is the ability to generously contribute material resources and/or money beyond the 10 percent tithe so that the church may grow and be strengthened. It includes the ability to manage money so it may be given to support the ministry of others.

HOSPITALITY—1 Peter 4:9–10

This is the ability to make others, especially strangers, feel warmly welcomed, accepted, and comfortable in the church family and the ability to coordinate factors that promote fellowship.

LEADERSHIP—Romans 12

This is the ability to clarify and communicate the purpose and direction ("vision") of a ministry in a way that attracts others to get involved, including the ability to motivate others, by example, to work together in accomplishing a ministry goal.

MERCY—Romans 12

This is the ability to manifest practical, compassionate, cheerful love toward suffering members of the body of Christ.

PASTORING (Shepherding)—Ephesians 4

This is the ability to care for the spiritual needs of a group of believers and equip them for ministry. It is also the ability to nurture a small group in spiritual growth and assume responsibility for their welfare.

PREACHING—Romans 12

This is the ability to publicly communicate God's Word in an inspired way that convinces unbelievers and both challenges and comforts believers.

SERVICE—Romans 12

This is the ability to recognize unmet needs in the church family, and take the initiative to provide practical assistance quickly, cheerfully, and without a need for recognition.

TEACHING—Ephesians 4

This is the ability to educate God's people by clearly explaining and applying the Bible in a way that causes them to learn; it is the ability to equip and train other believers for ministry.

WISDOM—1 Corinthians 12

This is the ability to understand God's perspective on life situations and share those insights in a simple, understandable way.

TELLING YOUR STORY

First, don't underestimate the power of your testimony. Revelation 12:11 says, "They have defeated [Satan] by the blood of the Lamb and by their testimony. And they did not love their lives so much that they were afraid to die" (NLT).

A simple three-point approach is very effective in communicating your personal testimony. The approach focuses on before you trusted Christ, how you surrendered to him, and the difference in you since you've been walking with him. If you became a Christian at a very young age and don't remember what life was like before Christ, reflect on what you have seen in the lives of others. Before you begin, pray and ask God to give you the right words.

Before You Knew Christ

Simply tell what your life was like before you surrendered to Christ. What was the key problem, emotion, situation, or attitude you were dealing with? What motivated you? What were your actions? How did you try to satisfy your inner needs? Create an interesting picture of your preconversion life and problems, and then explain what created a need and interest in Christian things.

How You Came to Know Christ

How were you converted? Simply tell the events and circumstances that caused you to consider Christ as the solution to your needs. Take time to identify the steps that brought you to the point of trusting Christ. Where were you? What was happening at the time? What people or problems influenced your decision?

The Difference Christ Has Made in Your Life

What is different about your life in Christ? How has his forgiveness impacted you? How have your thoughts, attitudes, and emotions changed? What problems have been resolved or changed? Share how Christ is meeting your needs and what a relationship with him means to you now. This should be the largest part of your story.

Tips

- Don't use jargon: don't sound churchy, preachy, or pious.
- Stick to the point. Your conversion and new life in Christ should be the main points.
- Be specific. Include events, genuine feelings, and personal insights, both before and after conversion, which people would be interested in and that clarify your main point. This makes your testimony easier to relate to. Assume you are sharing with someone with no knowledge of the Christian faith.
- Be current. Tell what is happening in your life with God now, today.
- Be honest. Don't exaggerate or portray yourself as living a perfect life with no problems. This is not realistic. The simple truth of what God has done in your life is all the Holy Spirit needs to convict someone of their sin and convince them of his love and grace.
- Remember, it's the Holy Spirit who convicts. You need only be obedient and tell your story.
- When people reply to your efforts to share with statements like "I don't believe in God," "I don't believe the Bible is God's Word," or "How can a loving God allow suffering?" how can we respond to these replies?

101

- Above all, keep a positive attitude. Don't be defensive.
- Be sincere. This will speak volumes about your confidence in your faith.
- Don't be offended. It's not you they are rejecting.
- Pray—silently on-the-spot. Don't proceed without asking for God's help about the specific question. Seek his guidance on how, or if, you should proceed at this time.
- In God's wisdom, choose to do one of the following:
  - Postpone sharing at this time.
  - Answer their objections, if you can.
  - Promise to research their questions and return answers later.

Step 1. Everywhere Jesus went he used stories, or parables, to demonstrate our need for salvation. Through these stories, he helped people see the error of their ways, leading them to turn to him. Your story can be just as powerful today. Begin to develop your story by sharing what your life was like before you knew Christ. (If you haven't yet committed your life to Christ, or became a Christian at a very young age and don't remember what life was like before Christ, reflect on what you have seen in the life of someone close to you.) Make notes about this aspect of your story below and commit to writing it out this week.

_____

_____

_____

Step 2. Sit in groups of two or three people for this discussion. Review the "How You Came to Know Christ" section. Begin to develop this part of your story by sharing within your circle. Make notes about this aspect of your story below and commit to writing it out this week.

_____

_____

_____

Step 2b. Connecting: Go around the group and share about a time you were stopped cold while sharing Christ, by a question you couldn't answer. What happened?

Step 2c. Sharing: Previously we talked about the questions and objections we receive that stop us from continuing to share our faith with someone. These questions/objections might include:

- "I don't believe in God."
- "I don't believe the Bible is God's Word."
- "How can a loving God allow suffering?"

How can we respond to these replies?

Step 3. Subgroup into groups of two or three people for this discussion. Review "The Difference Christ Has Made in Your Life" section. Share the highlights of this part of your story within your circle. Make notes about this aspect of your story below and commit to writing it out this week.

_____

_____

_____

Step 3b. Story: There's nothing more exciting than a brand-new believer. My wife became a Christian four years before I met her. She was a flight attendant at the time. Her zeal to introduce others to Jesus was reminiscent of the woman at the well who ran and got the whole town out to see Jesus.

My wife immediately began an international organization of Christian flight attendants for fellowship and for reaching out to others in their profession. She organized events where many people came to Christ, and bid for trips with another flight attendant who was a Christian so they could witness on the planes. They even bid for the shorter trips so they could talk to as many different people as possible. They had a goal for every flight to talk to at least one person about Christ, and to be encouraged by at least one person who already knew him. God met that request every time.

In her zeal, however, she went home to her family over the holidays and vacations and had little or no success. Later she would realize that she pressed them too hard. Jesus said a prophet is without honor in his own town, and I think the same goes for family. That's because members of your family think they know you, and are more likely to ignore changes, choosing instead to see you as they've always seen you. "Isn't this the carpenter's son—the son of Joseph?" they said of Jesus. "Don't we know this guy?"

With family members you have to walk with Christ openly and be patient. Change takes time. And remember, we don't save anyone. We just introduce them to Jesus through telling our own story. God does the rest.

Step 4. As a group, review *Telling Your Story*. Share which part of your story is the most difficult for you to tell. Which is the easiest for you? If you have time, a few of you share your story with the group.

Step 5. Throughout this study we have had the opportunity to develop our individual testimonies. One way your group can serve each other is to provide a safe forum for "practicing" telling your stories. Continue to take turns sharing your testimonies now. Set a time limit—say two to three minutes each. Don't miss this great opportunity to get to know one another better and encourage each other's growth too.

SERVING COMMUNION

Churches vary in their treatment of communion (or the Lord's Supper). We offer one simple form by which a small group can share this experience together. You can adapt this as necessary, or omit it from your group altogether, depending on your church's beliefs.

Steps in Serving Communion

1. Open by sharing about God's love, forgiveness, grace, mercy, commitment, tenderheartedness, faithfulness, etc., out of your personal journey (connect with the stories of those in the room).
2. Read one or several of the passages listed below.
3. Pray and pass the bread around the circle.
4. When everyone has been served, remind them that this represents Jesus's broken body on their behalf. Simply state, "Jesus said, 'Do this in remembrance of me' (Luke 22:19 NIV). Let us eat together," and eat the bread as a group.
5. Then read the rest of the passage: "In the same way, after the supper he took the cup, saying, 'This cup is the new covenant in my blood, which is poured out for you'" (Luke 22:20 NIV).
6. Pray, and serve the cups, either by passing a small tray, serving them individually, or having members pick up a cup from the table.
7. When everyone has been served, remind them the juice represents Christ's blood shed for them, then simply state, "Take and drink in remembrance of him. Let us drink together."
8. Finish by singing a simple song, listening to a praise song, or having a time of prayer in thanks to God.

Communion passages: Matthew 26:26–29; Mark 14:22–25; Luke 22:14–20; 1 Corinthians 10:16–21; 11:17–34.

PERFORMING A FOOTWASHING

Scripture: John 13:1–17. Jesus makes it quite clear to his disciples that his position as the Father's Son includes being a servant rather than power and glory only. To properly understand the scene and the intention of Jesus, we must realize that the washing of feet was the duty of slaves and indeed of non-Jewish rather than Jewish slaves. Jesus placed himself in the position of a servant. He displayed to the disciples self-sacrifice and love. In view of his majesty, only the symbolic position of a slave was adequate to open their eyes and keep them from lofty illusions. The point of footwashing, then, is to correct the attitude that Jesus discerned in the disciples. It constitutes the permanent basis for mutual service, service in your group and for the community around you, which is the responsibility of all Christians.

When to Implement

There are three primary places we would recommend you insert a footwashing: during a break in the Surrendering section of your group; during a break in the Growing section of your group; or at the closing of your group. A special time of prayer for each person as he or she gets his or her feet washed can be added to the footwashing time.

SURRENDERING AT THE CROSS

Surrendering everything to God is one of the most challenging aspects of following Jesus. It involves a relationship built on trust and faith. Each of us is in a different place on our spiritual journey. Some of us have known the Lord for many years, some are new in our faith, and some may still be checking God out. Regardless, we all have things that we still want control over—things we don't want to give to God because we don't know what he will do with them. These things are truly more important to us than God is—they have become our god.

We need to understand that God wants us to be completely devoted to him. If we truly love God with all our heart, soul, strength, and mind (Luke 10:27), we will be willing to give him everything.

Steps in Surrendering at the Cross

1. You will need some small pieces of paper and pens or pencils for people to write down the things they want to sacrifice/ surrender to God.
2. If you have a wooden cross, hammers, and nails you can have the members nail their sacrifices to the cross. If you don't have a wooden cross, get creative. Think of another way to symbolically relinquish the sacrifices to God. You might use a fireplace to burn them in the fire as an offering to the Lord. The point is giving to the Lord whatever hinders your relationship with him.

3. Create an atmosphere conducive to quiet reflection and prayer. Whatever this quiet atmosphere looks like for your group, do the best you can to create a peaceful time to meet with God.

4. Once you are settled, prayerfully think about the points below. Let the words and thoughts draw you into a heart-to-heart connection with your Lord Jesus Christ.

☐ *Worship him.* Ask God to change your viewpoint so you can worship him through a surrendered spirit.

☐ *Humble yourself.* Surrender doesn't happen without humility. James 4:6–7 says: "'God opposes the proud but gives grace to the humble.' Submit yourselves, then, to God" (NIV).

☐ *Surrender your mind, will, and emotions.* This is often the toughest part of surrendering. What do you sense God urging you to give him so you can have the kind of intimacy he desires with you? Our hearts yearn for this kind of connection with him; let go of the things that stand between you.

☐ *Write out your prayer.* Write out your prayer of sacrifice and surrender to the Lord. This may be an attitude, a fear, a person, a job, a possession—anything that God reveals is a hindrance to your relationship with him.

5. After writing out your sacrifice, take it to the cross and offer it to the Lord. Nail your sacrifice to the cross, or burn it as a sacrifice in the fire.

6. Close by singing, praying together, or taking communion. Make this time as short or as long as seems appropriate for your group.

Surrendering to God is life-changing and liberating. God desires that we be overcomers! First John 4:4 says, "You, dear children, are from God and have overcome . . . because the one who is in you is greater than the one who is in the world" (NIV).

JOURNALING 101

Henri Nouwen says effective and lasting ministry *for* God grows out of a quiet place alone *with* God. This is why journaling is so important.

The greatest adventure of our lives is found in the daily pursuit of knowing, growing in, serving, sharing, and worshiping Christ forever. This is the essence of a purposeful life: to see all these biblical purposes fully formed and balanced in our lives. Only then are we "complete in Christ" (Col. 1:28 NASB).

David poured his heart out to God by writing psalms. The book of Psalms contains many of his honest conversations with God in written form, including expressions of every imaginable emotion on every aspect of his life. Like David, we encourage you to select a strategy to integrate God's Word and journaling into your devotional time. Use any of the following resources:

- Bible
- Bible reading plan
- Devotional
- Topical Bible study plan

Before and after you read a portion of God's Word, speak to God in honest reflection in the form of a written prayer. You may begin this time by simply finishing the sentence "Father, . . . ," "Yesterday, Lord, . . . ," or "Thank you, God, for, ..." Share with him where you are at the present moment; express your hurts, disappointments, frustrations, blessings, victories, and gratefulness. Whatever you do with your journal, make a plan that fits you, so you'll have a positive experience. Consider sharing highlights of your progress and experiences with some or all of your group members, especially your spiritual partner. You may find they want to join and even encourage you in this journey. Most of all, enjoy the ride and cultivate a more authentic, growing walk with God.

PRAYER AND PRAISE REPORT

Briefly share your prayer requests with the large group, making notations below. Then gather in small groups of two to four to pray for each other.

Date: _____

Prayer Requests

_____
_____
_____
_____
_____

Praise Reports

_____
_____
_____
_____
_____

Prayer and Praise Report

Briefly share your prayer requests with the large group, making notations below. Then gather in small groups of two to four to pray for each other.

Date: _____

Prayer Requests

_____

_____

_____

_____

_____

Praise Reports

_____

_____

_____

_____

_____

Prayer and Praise Report

Briefly share your prayer requests with the large group, making notations below. Then gather in small groups of two to four to pray for each other.

Date: _____

Prayer Requests

_____

_____

_____

_____

_____

Praise Reports

_____

_____

_____

_____

_____

Prayer and Praise Report

Briefly share your prayer requests with the large group, making notations below. Then gather in small groups of two to four to pray for each other.

Date: _____

Prayer Requests

_____

_____

_____

_____

_____

Praise Reports

_____

_____

_____

_____

_____

Prayer and Praise Report

Briefly share your prayer requests with the large group, making notations below. Then gather in small groups of two to four to pray for each other.

Date: _____

Prayer Requests

_____

_____

_____

_____

_____

Praise Reports

_____

_____

_____

_____

_____

SMALL GROUP ROSTER

Name	Address	Phone	E-mail Address	Team or Role	When/How to Contact You
Bill Jones	7 Alvalar Street L.F. 92665	766-2255	bjones@aol.com	Socials	Evenings After 5

(Pass your book around your group at your first meeting to get everyone's name and contact information.)

Name	Address	Phone	E-mail Address	Team or Role	When/How to Contact You

LEADING FOR THE FIRST TIME
LEADERSHIP 101

Sweaty palms are a healthy sign. The Bible says God is gracious to the humble. Remember who is in control; the time to worry is when you're not worried. Those who are soft in heart (and sweaty-palmed) are those whom God is sure to speak through.

Seek support. Ask your leader, coleader, or close friend to pray for you and prepare with you before the session. Walking through the study will help you anticipate potentially difficult questions and discussion topics.

Bring your uniqueness to the study. Lean into who you are and how God wants you to uniquely lead the study.

Prepare. Prepare. Prepare. Go through the session several times. If you are using the DVD, listen to the teaching segment and *Leader Lifter*. Consider writing in a journal or fasting for a day to prepare yourself for what God wants to do.

Don't wait until the last minute to prepare.

Ask for feedback so you can grow. Perhaps in an e-mail or on cards handed out at the study, have everyone write down three things you did well and one thing you could improve on. Don't get defensive, but show an openness to learn and grow.

Prayerfully consider launching a new group. This doesn't need to happen overnight, but God's heart is for this to happen over time. Not all Christians are called to be leaders or teachers, but we are all called to be "shepherds" of a few someday.

Share with your group what God is doing in your heart. God is searching for those whose hearts are fully his. Share your trials and victories. We promise that people will relate.

Prayerfully consider whom you would like to pass the baton to next week. It's only fair. God is ready for the next member of your group to go on the faith journey you just traveled. Make it fun, and expect God to do the rest.

LEADER'S NOTES
INTRODUCTION

Congratulations! You have responded to the call to help shepherd Jesus's flock. There are few other tasks in the family of God that surpass the contribution you will be making. We have provided you several ways to prepare for this role. Between the *Read Me First*, these *Leader's Notes*, and the *Watch This First* and *Leader Lifter* segments on the optional *Deepening Life Together: Promises of God* Video Teaching DVD, you'll have all you need to do a great job of leading your group. Just don't forget, you are not alone. God knew that you would be asked to lead this group and he won't let you down. In Hebrews 13:5b God promises us, "Never will I leave you; never will I forsake you" (NIV).

Your role as leader is to create a safe, warm environment for your group. As a leader, your most important job is to create an atmosphere where people are willing to talk honestly about what the topics discussed in this study have to do with them. Be available before people arrive so you can greet them at the door. People are naturally nervous at a new group, so a hug or handshake can help put them at ease. Before you start leading your group, a little preparation will give you confidence. Review the *Read Me First* at the front of your study guide so you'll understand the purpose of each section, enabling you to help your group understand it as well.

If you're new to leading a group, congratulations and thank you; this will be a life-changing experience for you also. We have provided these *Leader's Notes* to help new leaders begin well.

It's important in your first meeting to make sure group members understand that things shared personally and in prayer must remain confidential. Also, be careful not to dominate the group discussion, but facilitate it and encourage others to join in and share. And lastly, have fun.

Take a moment at the beginning of your first meeting to orient the group to one principle that undergirds this study: A healthy small group balances the purposes of the church. Most small groups emphasize Bible study, fellowship, and prayer. But God has called us to reach out to others as well. He wants us to do what Jesus teaches, not just learn about it.

Preparing for each meeting ahead of time. Take the time to review the session, the *Leader's Notes*, and *Leader Lifter* for the session before each session. Also write down your answers to each question. Pay special attention to exercises that ask group members to *do* something. These exercises will help your group live out what the Bible teaches, not just talk about it. Be sure you understand how the exercises work, and bring any supplies you might need, such as paper or pens. Pray for your group members by name at least once between sessions and before each session. Use the *Prayer and Praise Report* so you will remember their prayer requests. Ask God to use your time together to touch the heart of every person. Expect God to give you the opportunity to talk with those he wants you to encourage or challenge in a special way.

Don't try to go it alone. Pray for God to help you. Ask other members of your group to help by taking on some small role. In the *Appendix* you'll find the *Team Roles* pages with some suggestions to get people involved. Leading is more rewarding if you give group members opportunities to help. Besides, helping group members discover their individual gifts for serving or even leading the group will bless all of you.

Consider asking a few people to come early to help set up, pray, and introduce newcomers to others. Even if everyone is new, they don't know that yet and may be shy when they arrive. You might give people roles like setting up name tags or handing out drinks. This could be a great way to spot a co-leader.

Subgrouping. If your group has more than seven people, break into discussion groups of three to four people for the *Growing* and *Surrendering* sections each week. People will connect more with the study and each other when they have more opportunity to participate. Smaller discussion circles encourage quieter people to talk more and tend to minimize the effects of more vocal or dominant members. Also, people who are unaccustomed to praying aloud will feel more comfortable praying within a smaller group of people. Share prayer requests in the larger group and then break into smaller groups to pray for each other. People are more willing to pray in small circles if they know that the whole group will hear all the prayer requests.

Memorizing Scripture. At the start of each session you will find a memory verse—a verse for the group to memorize each week. Encourage your group members to do this. Memorizing God's Word is both directed and celebrated throughout the Bible, either explicitly ("Your word I have hidden in my heart, that I might not sin against You" [Ps. 119:11 NKJV]), or implicitly, as in the example of our Lord ("He departed to the mountain to pray" [Mark 6:46 NKJV]).

Anyone who has memorized Scripture can confirm the amazing spiritual benefits that result from this practice. Don't miss out on the opportunity to encourage your group to grow in the knowledge of God's Word through Scripture memorization.

Reflections. We've provided opportunity for a personal time with God using the *Reflections* at the end of each session. Don't press seekers to do this, but just remind the group that every believer should have a plan for personal time with God.

Inviting new people. Cast the vision, as Jesus did, to be inclusive not exclusive. Ask everyone to prayerfully think of people who would enjoy or benefit from a group like this—then invite them. The beginning of a new study is a great time to welcome a few people into your circle. Don't worry about ending up with too many people—you can always have one discussion circle in the living room and another in the dining room.

For Deeper Study (Optional). We have included a *For Deeper Study* section in each session. *For Deeper Study* provides additional passages for individual study on the topic of each session. If your group likes to do deeper Bible study, consider having members study the *For Deeper Study* passages for homework. Then, during the *Growing* portion of your meeting, you can share the high points of what you've learned.

LEADER'S NOTES
SESSIONS

Session One The Promise Initiated

Connecting

1. We've designed this study for both new and established groups, and for both seekers and the spiritually mature. New groups will need to invest more time building relationships with each other. Established groups often want to dig deeper into Bible study and application. Regardless of whether your group is new or has been together for a while, be sure to answer this introductory question at this first session.

2. A very important item in this first session is the *Small Group Agreement*. An agreement helps clarify your group's priorities and cast new vision for what the group can become. You can find this in the *Appendix* of this study guide. We've found that groups that talk about these values up front and commit to an agreement benefit significantly. They work through conflicts long before people get to the point of frustration, so there's a lot less pain.

   Take some time to review this agreement before your meeting. Then during your meeting, read the agreement aloud to the entire group. If some people have concerns about a specific item or the agreement as a whole, be sensitive to their concerns. Explain that tens of thousands of groups use agreements like this one as a simple tool for building trust and group health over time.

   We recommend talking about shared ownership of the group. It's important that each member have a role. See pages the *Appendix* to learn more about *Team Roles*. This is a great tool to get this important practice launched in your group.

Growing

Have someone read Bible passages aloud. It's a good idea to ask ahead of time, because not everyone is comfortable reading aloud in public.

4. God tells Adam that he must not eat from the tree of the knowledge of good and evil. It is the only restriction placed on humans in the garden.

5. Allow the group to highlight what they notice from the text. Some things about God might be: God gives Adam responsibilities in the garden; God provides for Adam's need for food and water; God gives Adam a choice to obey or not; God expects obedience but also gives humans freedom of choice and the ability to think for ourselves; God gives commands and warns of the consequences of failing to obey, which show his love and concern; God cares about beauty, because his creation is beautiful; God cares about Adam's need for companionship.

6. Some things about Satan might include: Satan is deceptive; Satan misquotes and twists God's words; Satan causes Eve to doubt God's goodness; Satan takes a good motive of aspiring to be more like God and turns it toward disobedience.

7. At the heart of Satan's deception is questioning the reliability and goodness of God's word. Humanity's nature is to question God's faithfulness, especially when circumstances don't seem to make sense. If Satan can convince us to doubt God, then he has been successful in alienating us from him, inviting evil into our lives. Satan also tempts Adam and Eve to be like God, to take charge of their destinies apart from God.

8. We tend to run from situations and people, and even God, when we have done wrong. Even though we may know we have sinned, we fail to face it straight on. It's humiliating and frightening to face the truth about ourselves.

9. Even though we sin, God does not abandon us. He consistently loves us and provides for us, even when we don't live up to His standard for us.

10. This moment is the birth of shame, which is an emotion of feeling exposed as flawed or inadequate. They know the difference between good and evil, and disobeying God is evil—their sinfulness is exposed to view. They feel embarrassment, a sense that they need to hide from God what they have done. This shame over what is revealed inside us quickly transfers to shame about what is visible on the outside. This shame involves not only hiding from God, but hiding from one another. Their relationship is no longer fully open.

11. The group should be a safe place for sharing ideas, and group members will benefit from learning what other people think. Some people will struggle

with this; they won't see punishment as loving. But love, justice, and God's nature/character are his motives for the consequences of sin. Verse 22 reveals his motive: If they eat from the tree of life in the state they are in (guilty of sin and separated from relationship with God, spiritually dead), they will live in that state forever. God has a plan to bring them back into relationship with him, and he needs to protect them so the plan can be accomplished.

12. Be open to different ideas about how the judgments are manifested in society today. Some answers might be: We have to toil (not just work) to meet our needs and to survive; farming takes great effort; women experience labor pains in childbirth. Also, the curse on the land affects our whole planet.

13. The first part of the promise in 3:15 is that there will be a struggle between Eve's descendants and Satan (played out in the history of humankind, and especially between Satan and one of Eve's descendants). The second part of the promise is that one of Eve's offspring will crush the serpent's head—he will have victory over Satan. The rest of this study will provide more detail later, so help the group look forward to learning the answer if it isn't clear at this time.

14. God protects Adam and Eve from eating from the tree of life, which would cause them to live forever separated from God in their fallen state.

Developing

This section enables you to help the group see the importance of developing their abilities for service to God.

16. The intent of this question is to encourage group members to set aside some time to spend with God in prayer and his Word at home each day throughout the week. Read through this section and be prepared to help the group understand how important it is to fill our minds with the Word of God. If people already have a good Bible reading plan and commitment, that is great, but you may have people who struggle to stay in the Word daily. Sometimes beginning with a simple commitment to a short daily reading can start a habit that changes a life. The *Reflections* pages at the end of each session include verses that were either talked about in the session or support the teaching of the session. They are very short readings with a few lines to encourage people to write down their thoughts. Remind the group about these *Reflections* each week after the *Surrendering* section. Encourage the group to see the importance of making time to connect with God a priority in their life. Encourage everyone to commit to a next step in prayer, Bible reading, or meditation on the Word.

Sharing

Jesus wants all of his disciples to help outsiders connect with him, to know him personally. This section should provide an opportunity to go beyond Bible study to biblical living.

17. Encourage the group to observe their interactions during the coming week with the intention of using these observations next week in evaluating the people that God has placed in their lives that he might want them to share with or invite to small group.

Surrendering

God is most pleased by a heart that is fully his. Each group session will provide group members a chance to surrender their hearts to God in prayer and worship. Group prayer requests and prayer time should be included every week.

18. Encourage group members to use the *Reflections* verses in their daily quiet time throughout the week. This will move them closer to God while reinforcing the lesson of this session through related Scripture.

Session Two The Promise Demonstrated

Connecting

2. We encourage groups to rotate hosts/leaders and homes each meeting. This practice will go a long way toward bonding the group. Review the *Small Group Calendar* and talk about who else is willing to open their home or facilitate a meeting. Refer hosts to the *Leader's Notes, Leading for the First Time (Leadership 101)*, and the *Frequently Asked Questions (FAQs)* in the *Appendix* for help preparing for their turn at facilitating the group meeting.

   Rotating host homes and leadership, along with implementing *Team Roles* as discussed in *Session One* will quickly move the group ownership from "your group" to "our group."

Growing

If you are leading the group for the first time, refer to *Leading for the First Time (Leadership 101)* in the *Appendix* for help. Also, read through the *Introduction* in the *Leader's Notes* and the *Leader's Notes* for this session so you are prepared to lead the meeting. Don't forget to encourage people as they participate in the discussion and don't allow one person to dominate the discussion. Watch the time carefully and remember, it is not necessary that everyone answer every question in the Bible study.

4. Moving hundreds of miles was much more difficult then than now. Abram would cut himself off from the kinship network that was a person's source of identity and safety. His kin would protect him; strangers would treat him as an outsider. He was leaving familiar customs behind. Moving to a foreign country can be wrenching today, but then it was far more of a culture shock.

5. Like Adam, Abraham knows the command but doesn't have lots of information about God's reason for the command. God doesn't explain, he asks for trust. There's plenty of room for the tempter to raise doubts. But unlike Adam, Abraham eventually (at age 75—we don't know how long after his call this was) trusts and obeys. And he receives a blessing, in contrast to the curses that follow Adam's disobedience.

Abraham's obedience is a first step to fulfilling the promise made in Genesis 3:15. The promise in Genesis 12:2–3 will bring about blessing for all nations instead of the curse that Adam and Eve's disobedience caused. See the *Study Note* on the curse in *Session One*.

6. These aspects of God's promise to Abraham are significant to all humankind in the following ways:

A great name (v. 2): Abraham's name is revered by most people in the world, as he is viewed as the founding father of Judaism, Christianity, and Islam. Among Christians, he is viewed as the model for faith in God's provision of salvation (Rom. 4).

A great nation (v. 2): Through Abraham's descendants—Isaac, Jacob (Israel), and then Jacob's twelve sons—God created the twelve tribes of Israel, a nation that has endured for four thousand years.

I will bless/curse those who bless/curse you (v. 3): This plays out in the life of Abraham in Genesis 12–25. Many believe it plays out in the history of the Jews. It is certainly true of Christ, the full heir of this promise.

All peoples will be blessed (v. 3): Through Jesus Christ, Abraham's greatest descendant, all nations have been blessed with the opportunity of salvation (Matt. 1:1; Rev. 7:9–10).

7. Matthew 1:1 reveals that Jesus is physically descended from Abraham.

In Luke 1:55, Mary prophesies God's mercy to Abraham and his descendants through her child.

In Luke 1:71–75, Zechariah prophesies that his son, John the Baptist, will herald the salvation that fulfills the oath God swore to Abraham.

Jesus affirms in Luke 19:1–10 that salvation has come to the house of Zacchaeus because he too is a son (descendant) of Abraham and that the Son of Man came to seek and save that which was lost.

127

In Acts 3:13–15, Peter said God glorified his servant Jesus by raising him from the dead, the affirmation of the promise God made to Abraham to bless all nations through his offspring.

In Romans 4:13–16, Paul says the offspring of Abraham receive the promise through faith, not the law.

In Galatians 3:6–9, 14, Paul uses Abraham as evidence that righteousness, justification, and redemption all come by faith in Christ, so even the Gentiles can receive the promised Holy Spirit.

8. Through Jesus's death on the cross, all who believe receive the blessing of salvation. If you are Jewish, you are part of the great nation that God promises in 12:2. If you are not Jewish, you come from the "all peoples on earth" (12:3) who are blessed through Abraham's descendant.

9. Abraham didn't just believe things about God intellectually. His "faith" was trust expressed through action: leaving his homeland, going to the Promised Land, offering Isaac as a sacrifice when God asked him to.

10. Abraham is a model for acting in faith as he obeyed God even though "he did not know where he was going" (Heb. 11:8 NIV). God may send us into a workplace or a city or a family to do the works of Christ, and he asks us to do these things by faith.

Developing

11. For many, spiritual partners will be a new idea. We highly encourage you to try pairs for this study. It's so hard to start a spiritual practice like prayer or consistent Bible reading with no support. A friend makes a huge difference. As leader, you may want to prayerfully decide who would be a good match with whom. Remind people that this partnership isn't forever; it's just for a few weeks. Be sure to have extra copies of the *Personal Health Plan* available at this meeting in case you need to have a group of three spiritual partners. It is a good idea for you to look over the *Personal Health Plan* before the meeting so you can help people understand how to use it.

Instruct your group members to enlist a spiritual partner by asking them to pair up with someone in the group (we suggest that men partner with men and women with women) and turn to the *Personal Health Plan*.

Ask the group to complete the instructions for the WHO and WHAT questions on the *Personal Health Plan*. Your group has now begun to address two of God's purposes for their lives!

You can see that the *Personal Health Plan* contains space to record the ups and downs and progress each week in the column labeled "My Progress." When partners check in each week they can record their partner's progress in the goal he or she chose in the "Partner's Progress" column on this chart. In the *Appendix* you'll find a *Sample Personal Health Plan* filled in as an example.

The WHERE, WHEN, and HOW questions on the *Personal Health Plan* will be addressed in future sessions of the study.

Sharing

13. A *Circles of Life* diagram is provided for you and the group to use to help you identify people who need a connection to Christian community. Encourage the group to commit to praying for God's guidance and an opportunity to reach out to each person in their *Circles of Life*.

    We encourage this outward focus for your group because groups that become too inwardly focused tend to become unhealthy over time. People naturally gravitate toward feeding themselves through Bible study, prayer, and social time, so it's usually up to the leader to push them to consider how this inward nourishment can overflow into outward concern for others. Never forget: Jesus came to seek and save the lost and to find a shepherd for every sheep.

    Talk to the group about the importance of inviting people; remind them that healthy small groups make a habit of inviting friends, neighbors, un-connected church members, co-workers, etc., to join their groups or join them at a weekend church service. When people get connected to a group of new friends, they often join the church.

    Some groups are happy with the people they already have in the group and they don't really want to grow larger. Some fear that newcomers will interrupt the intimacy that members have built over time. However, groups generally gain strength with the infusion of new people. It's like a river of living water flowing into a stagnant pond. Some groups remain permanently open, while others open periodically, such as at the beginning and end of a study. If your circle becomes too large for easy face-to-face conversations, you can simply form a second or third discussion circle in another room in your home.

Surrendering

14. Last week we talked briefly about incorporating *Reflections* into the group members' daily time with God. Some people don't yet have an established quiet time. With this in mind, engage a discussion within the group about the importance of making daily time with God a priority. Talk about potential obstacles and practical ideas for how to overcome them. The *Reflections* verses could serve as a springboard for drawing near to God. So don't forget these are a valuable resource for your group.

Session Three The Promise Individualized

Connecting

1. Encourage group members to take time to complete the Personal Health Assessment and pair up with their spiritual partner to discuss one thing that is going well and one thing that needs work. Participants should not be asked to share any aspect of this assessment in the large group if they don't want to.

Growing

3. God promises Isaac, "I will bless you and will increase the number of your descendants for the sake of my servant Abraham" (26:24). This is the promise to make a great nation from him, and a key phrase is, "for the sake of my servant Abraham." God doesn't repeat here the promise to bless all nations through this family, but that promise remains in effect.

4. Jacob (Israel) prophesies that among his twelve sons, the scepter (a sign of royal authority) will go to Judah, and that it will remain in his family until he comes to whom it belongs—that is, until Jesus comes. Judah will be the tribe of kings.

5. Matthew 1:1–6 reveals David as from the lineage of Judah. He comes from the royal tribe descended from Abraham, Isaac, and Jacob. David is also an ancestor of Jesus. This genealogy doesn't name all of the fathers and sons, but only representative ones to show the line of descent. There were actually about 800 years between Judah and David.

6. David comes from the lineage of Judah, so now a descendant of Judah is king of Israel.

7. When God had established David's throne in peace, David decided to build a "house" (a temple) for the Lord. God told David not to build this house. Instead, God would build David a "house" (a dynasty). God did not let David build the temple but promised that his son Solomon would do so. God also promised that the kingship would continue through Solomon, and that God would establish this royal line forever (v. 13). Forever is a long time for a royal dynasty.

8. This king will bring light to those in darkness (confusion, suffering). He will bring joy to Israel. He will shatter the yoke they are carrying (as an ox wears a yoke when it drags a wagon). He will break the rod (power) of the one who oppresses them. He will have several startling names (v. 6). He will reign in endless peace and justice.

10. Peter points to Jesus's miracles, but most of all he points to Jesus's resurrection as evidence that Jesus has fulfilled Psalm 16, in which David wrote that the king's body wouldn't decay.

    Jesus has now ascended to reign beside his father, king not simply of an earthly kingdom of Israel but of the universe. He has received the Holy Spirit and now gives the Spirit to his followers. If we acknowledge him as king, he gives the Spirit to us.

11. We often have a very narrow perspective: What is God doing right now for me personally? God wants us to understand that we are part of a vast story, a plan he has been faithfully carrying out for thousands of years, a plan that involves not just us but people throughout the generations and across the globe. If our little life isn't going well, we sometimes think God isn't really God. That's self-centered. We need to see the bigger picture and find our place in it.

Developing

12. The group members should consider where they can take a next step toward getting involved in ministering to the body of Christ in your local church. Discuss some of the ministries that your church may offer to people looking to get involved, such as the children's ministry, ushering, or hospitality. Remind everyone that it sometimes takes time and trying several different ministries before finding the one that fits best.

13. Encourage group members to use the *Personal Health Plan* to jot down their next step to serving in ministry, with a plan for how and when they will begin.

Sharing

14. It is important to return to the *Circles of Life* and encourage the group to follow through on their commitments to invite people who need to know Christ more deeply through Christian community. When people are asked why they never go to church they often say, "No one ever invited me." Remind the group that our responsibility is to invite people, but it is the Holy Spirit's responsibily to compel them to come.

Session Four The Promise Incarnated

Growing

3. Jesus descended from the lineage of David. Jesus was born of a virgin mother. Jesus was born in Bethlehem. Jesus came out of Egypt. These

details about his origin are meant to show us that he really is the Messiah that the prophets looked forward to. They're also meant to show us that God planned Jesus's life and death from the beginning of time, that none of this was unforeseen, none of this was Plan B after Plan A failed.

4. Isaiah says over and over that the Messiah will be full of the Holy Spirit, who will give him wisdom and power. Jesus receives the Holy Spirit at his baptism and goes to his home town in the power of the Spirit. He announces that he is fulfilling Isaiah 61, and then he goes on to his ministry of heal-ing, caring for the poor, and eventually freeing people from the oppression of sin and death. Group members may not yet fully understand why the Spirit's role is so important, but they will as this study progresses. Jesus ministered as a man in the power of the Holy Spirit. Then he returned to the Father and sent the Spirit to us. He means for us to minister as humans in the power of the Spirit too.

5. The King focuses on restoring life, not taking it away. There's a place for vengeance against injustice, but at his first coming, Jesus offers healing and good news, a chance for the corrupt and cruel to repent. He comes in humility and service. All those are marks of the King and his kingdom, and we should live likewise.

8. Adam and Eve failed when they gave in to Satan and disobeyed God. This sin brought about separation from God and the curse on all creation. Jesus passed a similar test, resisting Satan's lies and attempts to manipulate. In so doing, he paved the way to the restoration of all creation through the salvation of humanity. Jesus has been called a second Adam because Adam is "a pattern of the one to come [Jesus]" (Rom. 5:14).

9. Group members might not know enough about the Old Testament to fully answer this. If not, suggest that they read Deuteronomy 1–9. Just as Jesus relived the test Adam faced, and did what Adam should have done, so Jesus relived the test Israel faced, and did what Israel should have done. The Israelites spent forty years in the desert because they doubted God, and then when they conquered the Promised Land, they were frequently faithless and so were only partly successful. They didn't learn what they should have learned in the wilderness: that God can be counted on; that he alone deserves trust and worship; that focusing on one's material needs alone is a drastic mistake. Jesus is what Adam and Israel should have been. He takes into himself all the tests and sins of human history, and gets things right this time.

10. The Old Testament frequently shows us the meaning of what Jesus says and does. Jesus didn't come in a vacuum; God spent two thousand years from the time of Abraham to the time of Jesus preparing a historical context for him to step into. The whole story is a unity, God's story of promising and sending someone to rescue us from the predicament we got ourselves

into at the beginning of human history. We need to see our lives as part of this larger story and trust a God who often takes centuries to work out his purposes. We need to not get impatient and self-focused.

Developing

11. Point the group to the *Spiritual Gifts Inventory* in the *Appendix*. Read through the spiritual gifts and engage the group in discussion about which gifts they believe they have. Encourage group members to review these further on their own time during the coming week, giving prayerful consideration to each one. We will refer back to this again later in the study.

Sharing

12. This activity provides an opportunity for the group to share Jesus in a very practical way. Discuss this and choose one action step to take as a group. Be certain that everyone understands his or her role in this activity. It might be a good idea to call each person before the next meeting to remind people to bring to the next session what is required of them.

    Designate one person to investigate where to donate items in your area. That person can also be responsible for dropping off the items.

13. Encourage group members to think about when they are shepherding another person in Christ. This could be simply following through on inviting someone to church or reaching out to them in Christ's love. Then have everyone answer the question "WHEN are you shepherding another person in Christ?" on the *Personal Health Plan*.

Session Five The Promise Fulfilled

Growing

4. We don't know what Jesus looked like before his arrest, but Isaiah suggests that his appearance might have been unremarkable. But certainly by the time he was flogged (beaten) and nailed to the cross, he was horribly disfigured.

    Jesus was mocked and tortured as he hung on the cross. But he may well have been despised and familiar with pain long before that. His family thought for a while that he was crazy (Mark 3:21). Throughout his ministry he was barraged with hostile questions and tests. His disciples didn't understand him. No one understood him enough to be a true friend. His cousin John the Baptist was killed. He spent most of his ministry among the poor, the sick, and the demon-afflicted.

5. These verses beautifully explain the atonement, in which Jesus took our sins on himself and suffered the full death penalty for them. It's full of paradox, him substituting for us: by his wounds we are healed.

6. Their charges of blasphemy and treason were false, trumped up. He was innocent, and they had no real evidence against him. He didn't dignify their charges by treating them as if they deserved honest reply.

8. Astonishingly, Isaiah foresaw not only the crucifixion, but also Jesus's resurrection and exaltation to the Father's side. Because he was raised, we will be also. Jesus overcame the penalty and sting of death; it no longer holds power over us.

9. With hindsight, it may seem obvious to us that the Messiah would be crucified, raised from the dead, and then exalted to a throne for an eternal reign of justice and peace. But Isaiah never says that the suffering servant and the king will be the same person. One suffers; the other reigns. For a long time the disciples saw what they wanted to see and tuned Jesus out when he tried to prepare them for his death.

11. Jesus has crushed the serpent (Satan) by undergoing death, the penalty Adam and Eve earned by their disobedience. Satan no longer has the power over us that he had before.

   Since death came through a man (Adam), the resurrection of the dead comes also through a man (Jesus) who brings spiritual life and relationship with God. Satan bruised Jesus's heel (a non-permanent wound) when he went to the cross, but in the resurrection Jesus crushed Satan's head (an eternal defeat) by overcoming his power over death.

12. The story of Jesus's resurrection isn't something his disciples made up after he was tragically executed. It took them completely by surprise, and nothing in their expectations (despite what he said) prepared them for it. But after the fact, it was clear that God had said centuries earlier that he had planned this death and resurrection. The crucifixion wasn't a mistake. It was planned for a remarkable purpose: to pay the price for our sin. Understanding God's long-range plan should help us trust him whenever things happen that we don't understand immediately.

Developing

13. If members of the group have committed to spending time alone with God, congratulate them and encourage them to take their commitment one step further and begin journaling. Review *Journaling 101* in the *Appendix* prior to your group time so that you are familiar with what it contains.

Sharing

16. It is important to return to the *Circles of Life* often, both to encourage the group to follow through on their commitments as well as to foster growth toward new commitments. Encourage the group this week to consider reaching out to their non-Christian friends, family, and acquaintances. Remind everyone that our responsibility is to share Jesus with others, but it is the Holy Spirit's responsibility to convict souls and bring forth change.

17. Discuss the implication of Jesus's mandate to take the gospel to the "ends of the earth" on the lives of believers today. Have each person consider the action steps listed and choose one to begin immediately as a way of doing their part in seeing this accomplished.

Session Six The Promise Realized in Believers

Growing

4. This is dramatic stuff. God pours out his Spirit not just on the Messiah, but on all kinds of people. The Spirit enables them to prophesy. He makes them see visions. Various other end-times things happen, such as wonders in the heavens, and darkness that obscures the sun and makes the moon blood-red.

5. The disciples need to wait to be baptized with the Holy Spirit. The Spirit will give them power to be witnesses about Christ to those who don't know what he's done, both nearby and all over the world.

6. The Holy Spirit is poured out, and the disciples prophesy (in the sense not of foretelling but of forth-telling the truth about Jesus). Power like the uncontrollable forces of nature is one implication of verses 2–3. Scenes like this will understandably make some group members uncomfortable. The Holy Spirit isn't always this dramatic, but as a beginning taste of what the Old Testament promises about the Holy Spirit, this is the place to start.

8. The Holy Spirit isn't just for the elite. In the Old Testament, only the rare prophets received the Spirit. Now that Jesus has risen from the dead, returned to the Father, and poured out the Spirit, the Spirit is for all believers.

9. This is the first time the apostles announce publicly that Jesus has risen from the dead, so a dramatic sign of the Spirit poured out is appropriate. Christians debate whether we should expect the Spirit will often, sometimes, or never do this sort of thing today.

11. Believers are being transformed into the likeness of Christ over time with ever-increasing glory. Glory suggests brilliance, beauty, and weight. This

glory comes from the Lord, who is the Spirit. "Lord" usually refers to Christ, or even the Father, but the title is appropriate for the Spirit too. He is God, and he is one and equal with the Father and the Son.

12. Some examples of the transforming work of the Holy Spirit in our lives include the new birth that makes us God's adopted heirs; the experience of being ruled by the Spirit and not by the flesh; being united in one body with other believers; having our character transformed so that we are less controlled by our faults and so that love, patience, etc. become stronger in us; having deeper discernment as to what is true or trustworthy; having understanding of biblical teaching; having boldness to share the message of Christ with others. The point is that it is normal for Christians to be transformed by the Spirit more and more.

Developing

14. This activity provides an opportunity for the group to share Jesus in a very practical way. Discuss this with the group and choose one action step to take as a group. Invite one person to volunteer to be the point person on this. They would investigate the action step you have chosen and report back to the group what they find out. For example, if you have chosen to do yard work, the point person would contact the church to find a needy family and schedule the work to be done. It is ideal that every member of the group participates, but don't wait until all schedules align before making a plan to follow through. Many times, waiting until eight or ten individuals are available can cause a plan to fizzle out entirely.

Sharing

15. Encourage group members to consider developing their salvation story as a tool for sharing their faith with others. Begin the process during your group time and encourage the group to complete the exercise at home. As leader, you should review the "Tips" section of *Telling Your Story* yourself in advance and be ready to share your ideas about this process with the group.

Surrendering

17. Have everyone answer the question "HOW are you surrendering your heart?" on the *Personal Health Plan*.

Session Seven The Promise Finalized

Connecting

2. Take a few minutes for group members to share one thing they learned or a commitment they made or renewed during this study. They may also want to share what they enjoyed most about the study and about this group.

   Be prepared to offer some suggested resources for answering questions that may arise from this study. Offer other Scripture that relates to the topics studied. Ask your pastor to suggest some helpful books or articles. Advise group members to schedule a meeting with a pastor to get answers to difficult questions. Whatever you do, don't let anyone leave with unanswered questions or without the resources to find the answers they seek.

Growing

3. Many eyewitnesses, including Paul, confirmed seeing Jesus alive in his resurrected body. The chief argument for disbelieving Paul is that bodily resurrection is impossible, so there must be another explanation. But bodily resurrection is impossible only by normal natural processes. The people who argue this way assume (but can't prove) that only natural processes exist. With no evidence, they simply rule out supernatural causes. They rule out God. Once we take that unprovable assumption away and admit the possibility that a creator God exists, then resurrection is possible. We then have to decide whether Paul and the other apostles are credible witnesses. Are they lying? (Why would they, given that there was no money to be made, and most of them were tortured and killed for the claim?) Are they self-deluded? (But Paul came to believe in Jesus's resurrection completely independent of the other witnesses, against his own personal interests and biases.)

4. Jesus's crucifixion paid the price for our sins and so reversed the judgment against Adam (and ultimately against all creation). His resurrection proved that he had destroyed Adam's punishment: death. "In Adam," all people died spiritually and were separated from God's presence because of Adam and Eve's sin. But because Christ took on the penalty of all humanity's sin, we become spiritually alive and enjoy a personal relationship with God (vv. 21–22). That's part of what being "in Christ" does for us.

5. If Christ wasn't raised, then he wasn't the Messiah. He didn't conquer death for us. He didn't win forgiveness of sins and eternal life for us. He was simply a misguided Jewish teacher, and all of Christianity is a delusion.

6. Christ's resurrection was the "firstfruits" (down payment) of the end-time resurrection of the dead. Jesus was the first resurrected person who continues to live; he is immortal. He was first, but those who are in Christ will rise

137

from the dead in immortality when we receive our glorified bodies. Then death will be destroyed, and Christ will reign over all that exists, except the Father. The Son is equal to the Father in being God, but he willingly submits to the Father in all things.

7. A seed must die and be planted in order to become a living plant. The seed grows into a different body than a seed. So it is with our human bodies. Resurrection is not the resuscitation of a corpse. Jesus's body now is different in ways we don't understand from the body he had before. But it is a body, material in some way. We're not talking just about immortal souls, but about immortal bodies. Glorified bodies are imperishable, glorious, not subject to weakness, and spiritual (which means permeated with the Spirit, not ghostly or immaterial). The seed, our body, must die before it can come to life (v. 36). God gives it a body as he determines (v. 38). The spiritual body is different than the earthly body.

8. The reception of our glorified bodies will mean the end of suffering and death.

9. Paul is clearly saying we will be material in some way. Humans are embodied beings, not just souls temporarily resident in bodies. The ancient Greeks to whom Paul was writing believed that souls were immortal, so he didn't have to write this much to convince them of that. He was trying to convince them to believe in immortal bodies, and they found that hard to take because they had a very low view of bodies. They wanted to shed their bodies, not have new ones.

10. Reincarnation is the belief that souls are transplanted from one body like the ones we already have to another body like the ones we already have. A person comes back to this earth with a body that ages and dies. Resurrection means coming alive again in a substantially transformed world with a substantially different kind of body. And we will be resurrected once, not reincarnated over and over.

11. When Christ returns, those who have died in Christ will be raised in imperishable bodies, and those who are still alive will be transformed immediately into glorified bodies. See also Philippians 3:20–21 and Romans 8:23.

12. There are many possible answers. For instance, whatever suffering we endure now, especially physical suffering, can be endured if we take the perspective that it is temporary. We are heading somewhere good. We can live with strong hope now.

DEEPENING LIFE TOGETHER SERIES

Deepening Life Together is a series of Bible studies that offers small groups an opportunity to explore biblical subjects in several categories: books of the Bible (*Acts, Romans, John, Ephesians, Revelation*), theology (*Promises of God, Parables*), and spiritual disciplines (*Prayers of Jesus*).

A *Deepening Life Together* Video Teaching DVD companion is available for each study in the series. For each study session, the DVD contains a lesson taught by a master teacher backed by scholars giving their perspective on the subject.

Every study includes activities based on five biblical purposes of the church: Connecting, Growing, Developing, Sharing, and Surrendering. These studies will help your group deepen your walk with God while you discover what he has created you for and how you can turn his desires into an everyday reality in your lives. Experience the transformation firsthand as you begin deepening your life together.